Garlic, Onion,
& Other Alliums

Garlic, Onion, & Other Alliums

Ellen Spector Platt

STACKPOLE
BOOKS

For my favorite garlic grower,
Jen P. Hopkins

Published by
STACKPOLE BOOKS
5067 Ritter Road
Mechanicsburg, PA 17055
www.stackpolebooks.com

Printed in China

10 9 8 7 6 5 4 3 2 1

FIRST EDITION

Cover design by Wendy Reynolds
Cover photography by Alan and Linda Detrick
Interior photographs by Ellen Spector Platt, unless otherwise noted.

Library of Congress Cataloging-in-Publication Data

Platt, Ellen Spector.
    Garlic, onion, and other alliums / Ellen Spector Platt.–1st ed.
        p.   cm.
        ISBN 0-8117-2891-9 (pbk.)
        1. Garlic.   2. Onions.   3. Allium.   4. Nature craft.   I. Title.
SB351.G3P44   2003
635′.26–dc21

                                                            2002155869

Contents

Preface

Garlic, onions, leeks, chives: How could we cook without them? How bland would be the flavor! How dull the aroma! These plants all belong to the botanical genus known as *Allium,* which also includes the flowering, or decorative, onions—those gorgeous balls and stars of perennial color. Flowering onions are becoming highly prized as ornamentals in the garden, and even culinary alliums are often intermixed in the flower border to help ward off insects and larger pests such as deer and rabbits (see chapter 4).

There are collectors of alliums, as there are collectors of orchids, mosses, or begonias, who seek to grow the rarest, the most challenging, the most obscure. Indeed, botanical collectors are not unlike those who accumulate Ming china or salt and pepper shakers. They all share in the thrill of the chase and the desire to acquire, and they all possess an intricate knowledge of the lore. Botanical gardens and research institutions send botanical collectors to unpopulated areas, rain forests, deserts, and mountains to bring back all types of plant species that may be unknown to the Western world, so that they can be studied and perhaps propagated for future use in home gardens.

LEFT: **Annabelle with yellow and blue allium ready for the vase.**

CHAPTER ONE

All the Alliums

The *Allium* species number at least 700, some say as many as 1,000, including both wild and cultivated types. The genus *Allium* is part of the lily (Liliaceae) family. These plants grow from either rhizomes or bulbs that form clumps, and they are perennial in their native habitat. The flowers grow in umbels at the top of strong stems, usually in a ball or oval shape, but occasionally in pendant form, and they are striking in border gardens. Umbels are umbrella-like structures that support numerous small flowers. The overall appearance of many alliums is of a strong, leafless stem with a sphere of flowers at the top. In fact, some of the larger flowering alliums are planted as curiosities or in children's gardens because of their resemblance to big lollipops. Each of the flowers on the umbel is small to tiny and may be bell shaped, cup shaped, or star shaped. Among the ornamental onions, it's not unusual to find 30 to 60 flowers in a ball on one stem. In some species, the umbel droops and there are many fewer flowers, giving a more graceful but less dramatic appearance.

One of the characteristics of alliums is the mild to strong smell of garlic or onions when the leaves are crushed. Also characteristic, but less important to most home gardeners, is the fact that each little flower in every species has six stamens. Sometimes the leaves, which come up from the bulb or rhizome, die back before the plant comes into bloom, leaving a space in the border which must be filled by other plants, but not by mulch.

LEFT: **Allium bulbs, stems, and flowers look pretty enough to eat.** PHOTO BY ALAN AND LINDA DETRICK

1

The Need to Grow Your Own

Home gardeners don't need to be convinced that the flavor of freshly harvested asparagus, peas, beets, and corn is incomparable. Eating these vegetables after they have languished on the supermarket shelves is like eating an alien species. Likewise, herb growers know that nothing will elevate a simple recipe more easily than a tablespoon or two of freshly snipped herbs, whether cut from a pot sitting on the kitchen windowsill or from a formal four-square herb garden.

The food varieties offered in the supermarket are usually those that ship best and have the longest shelf life, whether it's apples, tomatoes, or garlic. I was well into my 40s before it occurred to me that the papery white garlic from the A&P was not the only variety in the world. Hot peppers aren't all the same, garlic isn't all the same, onions aren't all the same—it's an obvious truth. If you want to enjoy the full range of flavors, you have to grow your own or go to a farm market or a garlic festival, where adventurous growers offer varieties based on flavor alone. If your 'Rocambole' garlic doesn't keep as long as some of the others, solve that problem by eating it up faster.

In addition to the flavor and the pleasure of eating your freshly pulled crop, grow alliums as companion plants to ward off pests and diseases from roses, carrots, and tomatoes (see chapter 5). Some of the stories border on folklore, but others are backed up by solid research findings.

Grow allium for health reasons. If you want to eat the dosage of garlic normally recommended as medicinal, it's a great help to the budget to grow your own. And you can grow it organically, ensuring that your "medicine" isn't being contaminated by unknown sprays.

Grow flowering onions for the pleasure of inviting different species into your home garden, for the contrast of form with other spiked plants, for the butterflies that hover nearby, and for the mouth-watering hint of aroma as you work in your beds. Generally hardy, easy to grow, animal resistant, and not prone to many diseases, the alliums are a treat for eye, nose, and mouth.

For convenience, I have separated the species into culinary and decorative types. This is not a botanical division, but purely a practical one to help you select your favorite species. There is much crossover between the two sections. For examples, I list chives and garlic chives in the culinary section, but they

Grow decorative onions as perennials in formal or informal settings.

Chives and top onions make an attractive combination.

are highly ornamental. The flowering alliums described in the decorative section also have an onion or garlic essence and are not poisonous, but they are not particularly known for their flavor. Certainly you can use flowers of decorative allium to garnish platters of food if that's what is in bloom at the moment.

Culinary Alliums

Chives
Allium schoenoprasum
Chives have hollow, grasslike leaves and usually pink, mauve, or lilac flowers, as many as 30 in a 1- to 2-inch ball at the end of the stalk. The plant grows from short rhizomes that send up clumps. Chives stand 12 to 24 inches, with the leaves remaining throughout the bloom period and beyond. Chives can be grown in zones 3 to 9; they like full sun but will tolerate some shade. Grow chives from seeds, buy the herb plants, or take divisions from your friends. In my garden, it's the first flower I cut for drying, usually in early May.

The leaves are usually chopped and used as a garnish for soups, salads, meats, and vegetables. The flowers are edible and more pungent than the leaves. They make a fine edible decoration in savory dishes and salads.

The flowers air-dry well if they are picked when mature. Bunch them by the handful in rubber bands and hang the bunches upside down to dry. Then use them in herbal and dried flower bouquets. Chives can also be used as a fresh-cut flower. The onionlike aroma is exceedingly mild. If you catch a tiny whiff when the stems are bruised, you will love it.

VARIETIES

A.s. 'Grolau': Developed to be grown indoors in greenhouses, this variety is a good choice if you like to keep pots of chives on your kitchen windowsill for your favorite recipes. It has a strong flavor and benefits from being cut regularly.

A.s. 'Forescate': The flower stems are 8 to 10 inches, with rich, rosy pink, clover-like flowers. The plant grows vigorously to 18 to 24 inches overall.

A.s. 'Sterile': Also called 'Profusion Chives' (source: Richters). This variety doesn't set seeds, so it blooms longer than common chives.

A.s. sp. 'Dwarf Chives': Good for rock gardens and the front of the border (sources: Well-Sweep and Sandy Mush).

Garlic Chives, Chinese Chives, Chinese Leeks

Allium tuberosum

A 1^1/$_2$- to 2-inch ball of usually white, starry flowers stands amidst the flat leaves of this hardy perennial (zones 3 to 8). A variety with mauve flowers is also available. The plant grows from rhizomes into clumps 10 to 20 inches tall and 12 inches wide, blooming in mid to late summer.

This species originally came from eastern Asia and is used in the cuisines of both Japan and China, where the flower buds are popular. Use the chopped strappy leaves in cooking as you would common chives for a spicy chive-garlic flavor. When cutting leaves for cooking, allow at least 2 inches to remain, to provide strength for the plant. The flowers make a fine decoration for salads, vegetables, meats, and cheeses.

Use the cut flowers among bunches of bright-colored annuals. If left to develop seed heads, the black seeds make an excellent con-

Garlic chives are a welcome addition to late summer beds, particularly if you enjoy volunteers in next year's garden.

trast to the tawny pods that hold them. Use them in dried bouquets and gar-
lands of any type. This species can be planted in containers.

Egyptian Top Onion, Tree Onion, Walking Onion
Allium cepa proliferum
The onions are formed at the top of fat, hollow stalks rather than underground,
like most other onions. The bulbils that form look like small shallots. They are
fine for flavoring and are good keepers. This species is perennial and hardy in
zones 5 to 9, but almost flowerless. The 2-foot stems often curve and bend
down to the ground under the weight of the bulbils, so new plants are formed
when the bulbils root.

I once used clusters of these bulbils in an allium wreath and was surprised
to see them send out small green shoots and grow on the wreath, even though
they seemed to be totally dry.

These onions are small enough to fit in the mouths of bottles to decorate
and flavor herbal vinegars. Or larger quantities can be pickled for a dinner
condiment.

Onions
Allium cepa
Onions are native to Asia. They found their way to Egypt through trade and
were considered an extremely important food plant in ancient times. The
daily rations of the slaves who built the pyramids included onions as a cheap
food. Alexander the Great brought onions from Egypt to Greece, and they
spread through Europe with his conquering armies. Since soldiers ate them
daily as part of mess, onions acquired the reputation for imparting bravery.

Onions are biennials, taking two years to flower and set seeds. Gardeners
who are impatient buy onion sets, or immature onions, which can be planted
in early spring and reach full maturity by late summer. More meticulous gardeners prefer to grow their own from seeds. But if the ground freezes in winter, you must pull the first year's small onions; store them in a cool, dry place;
and replant them in the spring—too much work for lazy folks like me. Sets
are more expensive, but for the home gardener, the difference in price is probably worth the savings in labor. In a child's garden, where a quick payoff is
crucial, be sure to plant sets for an early harvest. In fact, if you plant the sets

2¹/₂ inches apart, you can harvest every other one through the spring to savor as scallions or bunching onions. A major advantage of planting from seeds, however, is that there are far more varieties available, and some say that seed onions store better.

Onions are categorized by color, flavor, and size, but also by keeping or storage quality and by day length. Long-day onions are planted in the North, where the bulbs begin to size up when the days start getting shorter after the summer solstice around June 21. Short-day onions are planted in the South, because these varieties don't need such a long day to reach their maximum size. And middle-day onions are planted in the regions in between.

Your great-grandparents, grandparents, or even parents might have owned a root cellar, a little structure dug into the side of a hill that kept foods at a cool but not freezing temperature throughout the year. Potatoes, carrots, beets, onions, and other root vegetables were stored and used for up to a year until the new crop came in. Today, few people in cities and suburbs have the option of the root cellar, and even basements are often warm and dry, so other solutions to storage must be found. To cure onions after harvesting, cut off the stems

'Kelso Sweet' freshly dug and starting to "take the cure."

and roots and hang the bulbs in mesh bags or flat baskets. Select a cool spot, preferably around 50 to 55 degrees, that allows for air circulation. A dry atmosphere with low humidity is also necessary. Sometimes a garage serves the purpose over the winter, depending on the climate.

The gardener's decision at planting time will affect the dinner table six months hence. Select varieties that best serve your needs. The designation "storage onions" indicates those that last the longest. Others are listed for

Onions ready to be hung in a cool, dry spot.

medium- or short-term storage but may have the flavor you crave. Onions often become more pungent the longer they're stored.

VARIETIES

'Early Yellow Globe': An heirloom from the 1930s, this is a long-day onion, not for the South. As the name implies, it takes only 100 days to reach maturity.

'Elisa Craig Exhibition': If you're looking for a very large onion to submit to the county fair, try this almost pure white variety. Not a good keeper because of its sweetness. Not sensitive to day length.

'Red Wethersfield': An heirloom variety introduced circa 1800 and still going strong. A long-day variety for northern gardens with a deep red skin. Grown in Hancock Shaker Village, Pittsfield, Massachusetts, in a demonstration vegetable bed.

'Southport White Globe': This medium-sized, white-fleshed, white-skinned onion is a favorite of many judges. It is a long-day type.

'Torpedo Red Bottle': The name describes the onion—purple red, long, and thin. It is a short-day onion, better in the South than the North, with poor to moderate keeping qualities. This and other red bottle onions look beautiful in displays and centerpieces.

'Walla Walla Sweet': A favorite for over a century for its mild, sweet flavor; light brown skin; and juicy white flesh, but not a good keeper. Brought from Corsica originally, it is a long-day onion. In the Northwest, plant in early fall, winter over, and harvest in June.

'White Sweet Spanish': Sometimes called a hamburger onion. It has a 6-inch diameter, flattish bulb, and white skin and flesh. This long-day variety is used for eating raw and for making fried onion rings. Slightly pungent, with moderate storage qualities.

'Wonder of Pompeii': Very small, round onion for pickling, soups, and stews.

'Yellow Ebenezer': Pungent and an excellent keeper with a light brown skin.

'Yellow Granex': The mild, sweet onion grown in Vidalia County, Georgia, and marketed as the trademarked Vidalia onion. If you grow 'Yellow Granex' at home, odds are that the taste will be slightly different, possibly less sweet, unless you can simulate the same soil conditions. It is a short-day variety and not a good keeper.

Garlic
Allium sativum
Garlic has two main subspecies.

SOFT-NECK GARLIC
Allium sativum sativum
This is the variety found in most supermarkets, because it has the longest shelf life and ships well. There are usually two concentric rings of cloves in one bulb; cloves in the inner ring may be very small and hard to peel but fit well into a garlic press. Cloves are numerous (10 to 20) compared with those of stiff-neck garlic (see below). Most northern growers say the flavor is mild (i.e., deficient). It doesn't tolerate cold well (it's usually listed for southern gardens), but some varieties have been adapted by selection to colder regions.

This subspecies rarely forms a flower stalk. It's excellent for braiding because the stems are soft and there is no need to work to make them pliable, as with hard-neck garlic (see chapter 6).

HARD-NECK OR STIFF-NECK GARLIC
Allium sativum ophioscorodon
This is also called ophio garlic (short for the subspecies name) or top-set garlic. Hard-neck garlic sends up a flower stalk that makes a tight loop in some varieties and then forms a capsule at the tip holding tiny bulbils. Each bulb has four to ten cloves growing in a single ring around a woody stem. The little flower clusters don't set viable seeds, but the bulbils, about the size of a grain of wheat, can be saved and planted. They take three years in the ground before they are big enough to be dug for home use.

The loop of hardneck garlic is a wondrous thing to see, but must be cut off to force more strength into the bulb. Don't throw it away—add it to your next sauté or stir fry.

Hard-neck garlic is native to south-central Asia. It's usually recommended for zones 3 to 8. Bulbs can be stored for three to six months, making this variety less durable than soft-neck garlic.

Medicinal benefits have generally been attributed to hard-neck rather than soft-neck garlic. Many growers believe that the soft-neck types developed from hard-neck species that were selected because of the lack of a flower stem, better keeping quality, ease of growing, and greater productivity per acre.

TASTE

Garlic taste is rated on three dimensions:

1. Flavor: the degree of garlicky taste when eaten raw.

2. Heat or piquancy: how hot it is on your tongue when eaten raw.

3. Aftertaste: how long the flavor lasts.

Most taste testers agree that 'Rocambole' garlic, a hard-neck variety, has the best flavor. However, because this type is a short keeper, you generally have just three to six months to enjoy it, and six months applies only to the

Just before harvest, the garlic stems turn a soft brown.

highest-quality bulbs stored under optimal conditions. Ophio garlic in general may have the best flavor because it is more closely related to wild garlic than the soft-neck subspecies are.

When garlic is cooked, the heat dissipates, and only the flavor remains. That is why Julia Child's startling chicken recipe that calls for 40 cloves of garlic is so delicious—it's pure, concentrated flavor with the sting removed. When garlic is grown, all three taste characteristics vary depending on the water, sun, temperature, and soil. When garlic is stored, the taste also changes. It is mildest when first picked, then gets stronger. Old garlic is dry and almost flavorless and may become rancid.

VARIETIES

When selecting a variety, look for maturation date (early or late), color if important to you (some are pure white, and some have a reddish or purple cast), flavor, size of the bulbs, and number of cloves produced. Size is a consideration if you want to bake whole heads, then pull off the cloves. Conversely, if you use your garlic press frequently, you may want smaller cloves that will fit without peeling or cutting. Some cultivars are listed as easy peel-

Garlic will dry on screens, then the roots and stems will be trimmed.

ing, but note that the skins that make them easy to peel have an adverse effect on keeping quality; they tend to dry out more quickly.

A.s. ophioscorodon 'Rocambole': One of the most popular hard-necks for northern climes (down to Virginia), with some adapted to warmer areas. Requires a cold winter. Sometimes called "serpent garlic" because of the coiling shape of the flower scape, or stem. Often has purple stripes on the wrapper, six to eight cloves. Delicious flavor, but stores only three to six months

A.s. ophio 'Porcelain': Big, fat bulbs with thick wrappers; four to eight cloves per bulb. Handsome hard-neck garlic for display.

'Silverskin': Pure white soft-neck variety, typically found in supermarkets. It is an excellent keeper (up to a year) with small cloves and pliable stems, making it useful for braiding.

'Artichoke': Soft-neck type that is white tinged with purple; usually easy to grow. Has 8 to 40 cloves, with many smallish ones. For cooks who want only a hint of garlic, one of these small cloves might be enough. Keeps six to nine months. Named artichoke because the cloves grow in as many as four concentric rings, vaguely resembling an artichoke.

'Porcelain Music' garlic has the color of its namesake—almost pure white.

Leeks

Allium porrum

This nonbulbing form of onion is noted for its strong stalks and mild, sweet flavor beloved by cooks. Botanically, leeks are biennials that, left to their own devices, would flower and set seeds the second year. Most gardeners harvest at

LEFT: Leek flowers with their fairy caps popping. RIGHT: Although the flower is beautiful, the leek is too tough to eat at this stage.

the end of the first season, when leeks are most tasty. By the time they flower, most of the energy has gone into the blossom to set seeds before the plant dies, and the stems have gotten too woody to eat. Grow them as an annual, since the flower is not usually the desired portion. However, the flowers of the leek are beautiful in the garden, unfolding from the spathe like a fairy's cap in white, pink, or purple.

Seed varieties are usually sold with designations of early, maturing in 80 to 85 days; middle, maturing around 100 days; late, maturing in 130 to 135 days; and extra-late, maturing in 150 to 180 days. The extra-lates are very hardy; since they take five to six months to mature, they have to withstand some cold. Look for hardy varieties if you want the flowers.

Elephant Garlic
Allium ampeloprasum
(formerly *A. giganteum*)
This is not a true garlic but actually a type of leek. Many experts believe that it was culti-vated from the wild leek. It is sometimes called oriental garlic, a direct translation from the French *ail d'orient*.

People who find real garlic too strong are attracted to the mild flavor of elephant garlic. Bulbs are about twice the size of the largest true garlic. The name was popularized by a seed company that capitalized on the fact that to many Americans, bigger is better. Elephant garlic suddenly became a hot commodity when it had been languishing on the shelves. After all, roasted leeks on French bread just doesn't have the same cachet as roasted garlic. Elephant garlic stores longer than most garlic, even when the wrappers disintegrate and the cloves separate.

Ramps
Allium tricoccum
Collected by Amerindians and settlers for their strong onion flavor, ramps (also called wild leeks) are prized by a group of aficiona-dos in the hills of North Carolina and Ten-nessee, where they grow wild. The wild range

Ramps at the Union Square green market in New York City. Famous chefs from nearby restau-rants vie for the first harvest.

is from Nova Scotia to Georgia and west to Minnesota, according to the National Audubon Society's *Field Guide to North American Wildflowers.* Bundles of ramps make it to the specialty food markets and farm markets of big cities, and the *New York Times* food pages herald their arrival each spring.

Ramps grow 8 to 10 feet tall for early-spring flavoring in the pot. Leaves die down before the flowers bloom, as with many other *Allium* species. Flowers are cream colored. Edible parts are the stems, leaves, and small bulbs.

Two of the few companies that sell ramp seed are Richters and Sandy Mush (see sources on page 143).

Shallots

Allium ascalonicum (also *A. cepa* var.)

This is a smallish, reddish brown, mild-tasting bulb closer to onion than to garlic. Shallots (*eschalotes* in French) are beloved in French cooking but are rarely available except in specialty stores—one more reason to grow your own. In her famous book *Mastering the Art of French Cooking,* Julia Child gives recipes for shallot butter sauce with either red wine or white wine. Sub-

Bill Steiner digging his shallot crop in Orwigsburg, Pennsylvania.

stitutes in cooking are scallions or mild bunching onions. Use chopped shallots in soups, stews, and stuffings; use small shallots whole or halved in stir-fried dishes and casseroles.

Bunching Onions
Allium fistulosum
Bunching onions are thought to have been bred from the Welsh onion, a perennial that is sometimes grown for its lovely yellow flower. Its leaves can also be cut all year for pungent flavor.

Bunching onions are also called scallions, and they are available year-round in even the smallest and least imaginative supermarkets. Some people think of scallions as any onion pulled early in its growing cycle before the bulb starts to form, but true bunching onions will never form bulbs, no matter how mature they are or how tall the tops grow.

Bunching onions look like pencil-thin leeks. The bulb is no wider than the base of the leaves. The bottom few inches are white, and the tops are green. There are also deep purple or red varieties that show their color from the roots to 2 to 3 inches upward and make an interesting change from the ubiquitous white and green varieties.

Bunching onions are useful raw or cooked. The green part can be chopped and substituted for chives in recipes. Use scallions fresh or chop and freeze them in small plastic bags, as they don't store like bulbing onions.

Multiplier Onions
Allium cepa, aggregatum group
Multiplier onions are mild, sweet-tasting onions that form numerous (10 to 12) smallish bulbs underground on one plant. Multiplier onions must be cured and stored like bulb onions. They should last 6 to 12 months if unbruised and stored correctly in a cool, dry spot with good air circulation.

Decorative Alliums

Hundreds of flowering onions are offered in bulb catalogs and garden centers. There's a flowering onion for every spot in your garden—both in the ground and in containers. They are becoming hugely popular with gardeners because of their shape, size, and drama. They are true perennials that can last for years and often reseed. Some can be propagated by division. Another advantage is that they are usually rejected by hungry deer, groundhogs, mice, moles, voles, and other garden visitors.

Following is a selection of species representing different sizes, shapes, and colors. Consult the sources for a listing of on-line and paper catalogs to peruse and buy from. I've found all the sources listed to be very reliable.

A note about horticultural zones is in order. You can find yours easily by looking at the zone map included in almost every garden catalog or by calling your county extension agent. The zones listed here are for guidance only, and I tried to err on the conservative side. There are microclimates in any garden. For example, borders facing south backed by a stone or brick wall may provide a nice little solarium effect that allows planting up one hardiness zone. Conversely, in an unprotected area buffeted by cold winter winds, you may lose some plants even though your zone is listed as "safe." It's fun to experiment and try to push the boundaries a little, even if you may be unsuccessful.

A. *bulgaricum* just had a name change, but most gardeners still think of it as an allium, and a beautiful one at that.

Allium bulgaricum (syn. *Nectaroscordum siculum bulgaricum*)

Tall 36-inch stems with charming, bell-shaped, mostly drooping flowers. Interior of white flower tinged rose with a green throat. This bulb has been reclassified as *Nectaroscordum*, but most people know it by its former genus, *Allium bulgaricum*. Zones 6 to 8.

Allium caeruleum (syn. *A. azureum*)

One of the smaller alliums; grows 12 to 18 inches high. Should be planted in a larger grouping. True blue flowers grow in balls about 1 inch across with 30 to 50 star-shaped florets.

Allium carinatum pulchellum (keeled garlic)

Usually purple in color, but there is a white variety as well. Blooms are drooping, 1-inch bell-shaped flowers; plants grow 12 to 24 inches tall. Leaves are a lovely silvery blue, but many die back by flowering in midsummer. Develops large clumps of bloom over the years. Sometimes called *A. pulchellum,* but this is inaccurate. Heirloom, dating to 1810. Zones 5 to 8.

Allium cernuum (nodding onion, swamp onion, wild garlic)

Light pink to deep magenta flowers. Native to the Allegheny Mountain regions, where it blooms in July and August. Bell-shaped, drooping flowers are delicate and charming. Heights vary as this species adapts to different locales. Beware of look-alike plants without the characteristic odor, which are highly poisonous to eat. Zones 4 to 8.

Allium christophii (syn. *A. albopilosum*) (stars of Persia)

Blooms in late June to July, with shimmering amethyst flowers on heads 6 to 10 inches in diameter. Stems are fairly short relative to the

The true blue allium (*A. caeruleum*) is perfect for small fresh arrangements.

size of the head—12 to 18 inches tall. Leaves wither before flowers bloom. Makes a beautiful dried seed head in everlasting arrangements. Zones 4 to 8.

Allium flavum (small yellow onion)

Relaxed, yellow, bell-shaped florets, up to 60 on one head—an unusual color among *Allium.* Prominent stamens add to the texture. Blooms in June and July. Grows 12 inches tall. Recipient of the Award of Garden Merit by the Royal Horticultural Society. Zones 4 to 8.

LEFT: Planted among cat mint, the star of Persia can really shine. RIGHT: *A. giganteum* glistens in this variety, 'Mt. Everest.'

Allium giganteum (giant allium)

Up to 50 star-shaped lilac florets cover a 6-inch-diameter ball on a single straight stem. This 36 to 48-inch plant comes into bloom in late spring–early summer, by which time the foliage looks very unsightly. Plant giant allium among other tall perennials with large foliage both to keep it in scale and to hide the yellowing leaves. Heirloom giant, circa 1883. White forms, 'Mt. Everest' and 'White Giant', have a similarly large and dramatic appearance. Zones 5 to 7.

Allium 'Gladiator'

Flower balls are 6 inches across with up to 50 star-shaped florets, rose-purple in color. Blooms in May and June. Stands 24 to 36 inches tall. Some think it is a cross between *A. aflatunense* and *A. macleanii.* It has one parent in common with 'Globemaster'. Zones 5 to 8.

Allium 'Globemaster'

One of the biggest flower heads—up to 10 inches in diameter—consisting of violet star-shaped flowers. Plant grows 24 to 36 inches tall. Foliage remains green. Cross between *A. christophii* and *A. macleanii.* Zones 5 to 8.

Allium karataviense (Turkestan onion)

The leaves are an unusual feature of this plant. They are wide and recurved and usually have a red edge. The foliage is still lovely when the flowers bloom. Flowers are white to pale pink spheres 5 inches across, with up to 50 florets in each ball. Tolerates some shade. One of the Heirloom varieties, dating from 1876. Recipient of the Award of Garden Merit by the Royal Horticultural Society. Zones 5 to 9.

A. 'Globemaster', another giant, appears in a mass planting in Wave Hill's Wild Garden.

A. moly 'Jeannine' surprises with its yellow color and loose form.

Allium 'Lucy Ball'

Dark lilac, softball-size florets bloom in early summer. Tall stems reach 36 to 48 inches. Zones 3 to 8.

Allium macleanii (syn. *A. elatum*)

Rosy pink florets on balls that are 3 inches across, atop strong 2-foot stems. Attractive foliage. A parent of both 'Globemaster' and 'Gladiator'. Zones 4 to 8.

Allium moly (lily leek)

This small yellow allium will grow in dry shade. Blooms in May. It grows 12 to 18 inches tall, with upright clusters of up to 30 starry florets, 2 inches across. Naturalizes easily. *A. moly* 'Jeannine' has larger umbels. Zones 4 to 8.

Allium neapolitanum (Naples garlic)

White star-shaped flowers with green centers and prominent stamens form a 2- to 3-inch ball. Grows 12 to 20 inches tall. Excellent cut flower; fragrant. Often dyed in the floral trade. Heirloom, introduced circa 1828. Zones 6 and 7.

A. 'Purple Sensation' is one of the most popular flowering alliums.

A. 'Purple Sensation', with a mass of individual florets, is stunning in close-up.

Allium nigrum (syn. *A. multibulbosum*)

Blooms in late spring, with 20 to 35 silvery florets with green centers on 3- to 4-inch balls. Grows 18 to 26 inches tall. Blooms in late spring to early summer. Long-lasting perennial. Zones 4 to 7.

Allium oreophylum (syn. *A. ostrowskianum*)

Native to mountain regions, making it excellent for well-drained rock gardens. Short, 10-inch purple blooms in loose clusters. *A. oreophylum* 'Zwanemburg' has received the Award of Garden Merit by the Royal Horticultural Society. I have a hard time finding this variety in the United States. It has a carmine red flower head with clusters of 10 to 15 bell-shaped flowers. Zones 4 to 8.

Allium 'Purple Sensation'

Blooms in late spring on 30- to 36-inch stems. Four-inch balls of densely packed purple flowers with a reddish cast. Not an orphan, but parents in dispute; very popular nevertheless. Zones 4 to 7.

Allium rosenbachianum

Up to 50 reddish purple star-shaped florets on a 3- to 5-inch globe. White or purple stamens are prominent. Stems are 3 to 4 feet. Blooms in late spring. Heirloom, dating to 1884. Zones 5 to 7.

Allium roseum (rosy flowered garlic)

Blooms are white to pale pink on a 2-inch ball. Late-spring bloomer growing 10 to 15 inches tall. Long-lived in the garden. Often forms bulbils that self-propagate in the garden—a bonus to my way of thinking, but purists may disagree. Heirloom, introduced circa 1753. Zones 5 to 8.

Allium schubertii

Florets are loose and spidery, giving the flower a more relaxed look than the rigid lollipop of many alliums. Has extra flowers that shoot out like stars—a galactic look. Grows 12 to 24 inches. Can be forced indoors in colder climates. Leaves start to die back as flower blooms. Heirloom, circa 1843. Zone 7 to 9.

Allium senescens glaucum (silver corkscrew chives, curly chives)

This small allium has silvery leaves with a bluish cast, which often curl and spiral. At 6 to 8 inches tall, it works well in a rock garden or in containers where its form can show off. The flowers are pale pink to lavender and small; the spherical umbels are about the size of a quarter. Blooms in mid to late summer. Zones 5 to 9.

Allium sphaerocephalon (drumstick allium)

Beloved by florists for its dense, egg-shaped flower head with up to 40 deep burgundy florets, as well as for its long vase life. This variety

A. schubertii is tender, so enjoy it as a forced bulb north of Zone 7.

A. schubertii opens in a loose starburst display.

will naturalize in the garden. Grows 24 inches high. Blooms in early to mid-summer. Zones 5 to 9.

A. s. 'Hair' has the same purplish florets with wild green filaments flying from the center—drumstick allium having a bad hair day (source: Van Dycks).

Allium thunbergii 'Ozawa' (October onion)

The main advantage of this allium is that it blooms in late October into November, when most plants in the North are finished. Violet-pink florets on 8- to 10-inch flowers; leaves are narrow and flat. Suitable for partial shade. The size of the plant makes it excellent in the rock garden. Native of Japan. Zones 2 to 8.

Allium triquetrum (three-cornered leek)

Good for naturalizing in shade, and tolerates some moisture in the soil. Bell-shaped flowers are cream colored and droopy, giving them a graceful appearance. Grows 16 inches tall. Heirloom, circa 1789. Zones 4 to 8.

Allium unifolium

Pink flowers loosely arranged on 12-inch stems. This versatile allium can grow in sun or partial shade, and it is one of the few that tolerates a moist soil. Blooms in late spring. Native to California and Oregon. Zones 4 to 8.

LEFT: Drumstick allium is a favorite both in the garden and in arrangements. RIGHT: *A. unifolium*, one of the small, less showy alliums, is a favorite of some gardeners for those very qualities.

Allium zebdanense (Lebanon onion)

An unusual allium because it actually prefers a little shade, particularly from intense afternoon sun. Blooms in late April to mid-May in charming, loose clusters of six to ten white flowers. Perfect for dry woodlands. Goes dormant soon after blooming, and the plant seems to disappear until the following year. Zones 5 to 8.

CHAPTER TWO

History and Folklore of Alliums

According to an Islamic legend, when Satan left the Garden of Eden, having caused the fall of man, garlic sprang up where his left foot had been and onions where his right foot had been. These plants were thought to have magic powers.

Other legends support the theory that a clove of garlic worn around the neck wards off witches, werewolves, demons, and the evil eye. During the 1930s, a friend of mine from Brooklyn was made to wear a clove by her Bubbe as protection from the devil. And everyone knows that vampires—those creatures that rise from the dead at night to suck the blood of their victims—can be repelled by garlic worn around the neck. Some say that garlic hung from windows and doors also does the trick.

As we snicker, confident of our superior wisdom, we should remember vampire bats. These all-too-real creatures of the family Phyllostomidae inhabit tropical regions of the Americas and actually do bite other creatures and extract blood. Would garlic prevent such attacks? The use of garlic in gardens to ward off deer, rabbits, and other mammals suggests that garlic may be a deterrent.

Leeks, onions, and garlic have been a food of the poor, and leeks were known as a food of humility. However, Pliny records that the emperor Nero was very fond of leeks and that after his death he was derided by the epithet *Por-*

LEFT: Garlic chives in bud at the Strawbery Banke Museum in Portsmouth, New Hampshire. The gardens include beds with chamomile, hyssop, Russian sage, boxwood, and a wide variety of other plants.

Garlic wreath from Mud Road Farm in New York.

rophagus, or "leek eater." Leeks were revered in antiquity because they were thought to impart bravery to soldiers who wore them and to prevent injury. The Roman legions planted them in conquered territories for just this purpose. As they moved northward, the plant became popular in other locales.

Allium ascalonicum, a variant of shallot, was named after the city of Escalom in Palestine. The ancient Greek historian Herodotus reports that an inscription in the Great Pyramid of Cheops states that 1,600 talents of silver were paid to provide construction workers with onions, garlic, and radishes to sustain them while building this tomb, which was completed around 2680 B.C.E. Both onions and leeks grew wild in Egypt and were probably originally brought there in trade from central Asia.

The ancient Greek physician Dioscorides, who served Nero's army in Rome, noted in his five-volume tome that "garlic cleans the arteries." At that time, arteries were thought to transport air, not blood. Excavations of ancient Greek temples have identified garlic from 1400 to 1800 B.C.E. (Rivlin).

Onions are often seen in Egyptian tomb paintings and in the mummies themselves. "Whole onions were placed in the armpits, eye sockets, and bodily cavities, as well as the folds of the wrappings perhaps in the belief that the odor would stimulate the dead into breathing." (Strouhal, p. 128). Another reason might have been to keep wild animals from disturbing the mummies. When King Tutankhamen's tomb, dating from circa 1350 B.C.E., was excavated in 1922, garlic was identified among the plant matter (Rivlin).

The Old Testament of the Bible recounts that when Moses led the Jews out of Egypt to wander in the desert, they fed upon manna from heaven, but "the children of Israel wept. . . . We remember the fish which we did eat in Egypt freely, the cucumbers and the melons, and the leeks and the onions and the garlic; but now our soul is dried away and there is nothing but this manna before our eyes" (Numbers 11: 4–6). The Talmud, a book of Jewish commentary from the second century, reports that garlic was used for the treatment of infections and parasites (Rivlin).

Allium tuberosum (garlic chives or Chinese chives) was mentioned as food in the Chinese calendar in 2000 B.C.E. Garlic was used as a food preservative, as an aid to respiration and digestion, and to kill parasites. Kuhn and Winston reported that "Sanskrit records document use of garlic 5000 years ago" (p. 143).

Two thousand years ago, a medical text in India recommended doses of garlic for heart disease and arthritis. Reports of garlic use in medicine as either a preventive or a cure for disease continued through the Middle Ages and Renaissance, although in some instances, eating the plant was limited to the lower classes. Such important medical figures as St. Hildegard von Bingen, abbess of Rupertsberg in the twelfth century, and Pietro Mattiole of Siena in the sixteenth century recommended the bulb (Rivlin).

Settlers brought garlic to the American continent, but there are indications that wild garlic was already growing there and that the Indians were using it for medicinal purposes as well as for cooking. Wild onions were eaten by Native Americans raw, steamed, and dried and were mentioned in the journals of Lewis and Clark as a poultice and to prevent gas. Angier reported that the Dakotas and the Winnebagos "crushed wild onion and applied it to bee, wasp, hornet, and other insect bites with what was said to be marked success in reducing swelling and pain" (p. 294). The Cheyennes used crushed bulbs and stems applied as poultices to carbuncles and boils, both before and after lancing. The juice may have been applied by soaking clean sphagnum moss in diluted wild juice. A wild onion syrup boiled down with a sweetener, perhaps maple syrup, was used for croup, coughs, and colds in infants, children, and adults. Juice was "dropped in the ear to relieve aching and ringing noises" (Angier, p. 295). Juice from ramp bulbs was also used by American Indians and then settlers to rub on insect bites to relieve the itch and sting (National Audubon Society).

Some say that when the early Saxons invaded Wales in the sixth century, fighters for the homeland grabbed leeks from the fields before they ran out to

Firm, unblemished purple and white onions with a strand of dried peppers.

fight and placed them on their hats or jackets. That way, they would be able to identify the leekless enemy. When the invasion was repelled, leeks became the national flower of Wales. They were sported on March 1 to honor St. David, the patron saint of Wales, in memory of the brave fighters in that war. Others say that the custom started later, in the twelfth century, when the English invaded Wales on their way to conquer the more desirable land of Ireland. Although the English typically marched in uniform, a canny captain decreed that they should dress like the Welsh to confuse the homeland defenders. Getting word of this, the Welsh leader told his men to pin a leek or a daffodil from the fields on their clothing to identify themselves. Nevertheless, the English held sway, and the ensuing truce forced Wales to become part of England.

Shakespeare's *Henry V* includes a scene between the English Captain Fluellen and the soldier Pistol, wherein Pistol is forced to eat a leek as punishment for acting like a "knave." Anne W. Scott wrote to me that as a college student she "saw Albert Finney as a young repertoire actor playing that role of Pistol. He ate a raw leek at every performance, six evenings and two matinees. Don't know how he did it." She also reports that as a small girl in the 1950s, she wouldn't dream of going to school in Cardiff without her leek or "daff" pinned to her dress on St. David's Day. You must "wear a leek in your cap but be sure to have one in your heart," she says.

Garlic, like leeks, was also thought to impart bravery, strength, and invincibility to soldiers. It is said that Alexander the Great fed onions to his troops to bestow bravery. Animals are also braver for eating garlic. Mrs. Grieve in her book *A Modern Herbal* quotes earlier legends that "cocks fed on garlic are most stout to fight, and so are horses" (p. 343).

A European tale claims that if a man chews a garlic clove just before a race, no one will get ahead of him. A related legend applies to horses. Hungarian jockeys would attach a piece of garlic to the harness so that other horses would smell it and fall away, leaving the garlicky horse to run alone.

CHAPTER THREE

Medicinal Uses of Alliums

The bulb of the garlic plant, rather than the stem, flower, or leaf, contains the most active ingredients: vitamins A and C, potassium, phosphorus, selenium, amino acids, and between 23 and 100 sulfur compounds, depending on which expert you believe. When garlic is cut, minced, or chopped, the active ingredient allicin is released in an enzymatic reaction. The longer it is cooked, the less odor there is, and some think the less physiological benefit. The onion bulb is less potent than garlic but contains many of the same ingredients.

Louis Pasteur, the father of the germ theory of disease and a towering figure in modern medicine, showed in his research in the mid-nineteenth century that a distillate of garlic inhibited the growth of bacteria in the laboratory. As a result of Pasteur's discoveries, garlic was used to prevent or reduce bacterial wound infections in World War I. The antibiotic effect is thought to be strongest if the cut clove is placed directly on the infected tissue. By World War II, when penicillin and sulfa drugs were available to the U.S. armed forces, garlic was known as "Russian penicillin." It was used by the Red Army when it ran out of modern drugs.

Home Remedies

My Polish friend Ewa swears by two home remedies for coughs due to colds. Wrinkling her nose and making a bitter face, she described how her mother would cut a regular peeled onion in thin slices, then sprinkle one teaspoon of

LEFT: Wild ramps were once used as a poultice to treat insect bites and skin infections.

Fresh onion juice has been used as part of a weight-loss regimen.

sugar over the slices spread on a plate. After about two hours, she squeezed the onions by hand and collected the juice. It was this very strong, smelly juice that Ewa had to drink if she had a cough. Each day a new onion with sugar produced a spoonful of medicine that was dispensed until the cough went away.

To prepare the second remedy, put a cup of milk in a saucepan with two to three garlic cloves squeezed in a press. Add one teaspoon of butter and drink it as hot as possible. You can add a spoonful of honey if desired. This helps loosen the cough and reduce the buildup of phlegm in the lungs. Moving from Poland to Queens, New York, in no way reduced Ewa's reliance on these remedies, which she administers to her eight-year-old as needed.

Another friend from the Basque region in northern Spain reports that his Abuela dosed her pinworm-infested grandchildren with crushed cloves of garlic used as rectal suppositories. He related this memory from childhood when he was in his 50s. I've since heard of using one clove of crushed garlic dispensed in a dog's food for the same purpose.

Many believe that garlic cures yeast infections, and one writer swears that one clove of crushed garlic used as a vaginal suppository is easier and cheaper than pharmaceuticals used the same way.

Here are other remedies that some people accept as fact, but read on for a discussion of the hard data to support these claims (see page 41).

- Garlic "purifies the blood."

- Garlic and onions reduce clotting, so they reduce the risk of heart attack and stroke.

- One clove of garlic or half an onion a day reduces cholesterol and blood pressure significantly (Duke, p. 259).

- Garlic and onions are diuretics and good for kidney and bladder problems.

- Disulfides in garlic and, to a lesser extent, onions kill parasites that cause malaria.

- Garlic protects against the plague and leprosy. (It was a major ingredient in "four thieves vinegar," which said thieves dosed themselves with as they robbed the sick and dying during the plague.)

- Garlic is a cold and flu preventive. An active compound, the antiseptic allicin, goes to the lungs, as anyone breathing garlic hours after consumption can attest.

- Chicken soup replete with garlic and onion flavoring can cure or shorten the duration of colds.

Elephant garlic (rear), shallots (right), garlic cloves and even seed heads (left) have been used for centuries to ward off a long list of maladies.

- In traditional Chinese medicine, garlic is used to warm the kidneys and stomach and to treat incontinence, impotence, and sore backs and knees. Seeds of garlic chives *(Allium tuberosum)* are used as a tonic.

- Garlic and onions can be used as calmatives for nervous disorders and to treat headaches, asthma, indigestion, snakebites, tapeworm, and colic.

- Poultices of chopped garlic or onions on wounds can prevent infection. However, some people's skin is sensitive to the active compounds in alliums.

- Age spots and freckles can be lightened with a poultice of onion juice and vinegar or lemon juice.

- Burns can be treated with poultices of onion juice and salt (ouch!).

- Three cloves of minced garlic taken in juice every two hours is effective for pinworm, roundworm, *Giardia,* and other parasites.

- Fresh onion or garlic juice is effective in a weight-loss diet.

- The list of treatments in *The Green Pharmacy* (Duke) runs from *A* to *Y,* allergies to yeast infections. Dosing for a vaginal yeast infection includes up to 12 cloves of raw chopped garlic taken two to three times a day in juice (p. 463). (Draw your own conclusions about palatability and safety, but read about possible side effects on page 42.)

- The same antiseptic properties make garlic the herb of choice for athlete's foot: Crush two to three cloves in a footbath of warm water and rubbing alcohol (Duke, p. 68).

- Mrs. Grieve recommends onions macerated in Hollands gin as a cure for gravel and dropsy, and an application of roasted onion for tumors or earache (vol. 2, p. 599).

- The West Nile virus is spread by mosquitoes in the United States, and it can be fatal. People in affected locales are turning to home remedies such as garlic both to kill the organism causing the disease and to keep mosquitoes from biting. Garlic sprays on the skin are being used instead of DEET, although garlic is irritating to some.

- Garlic is effective against pulmonary infections such as whooping cough and bronchitis. It's antibiotic properties extend to tuberculosis, anthrax, cholera, staph and yeast infections, dysentery, and typhus.

- Garlic prevents the development and spread of cancer, increases overall resistance to disease and immunity, renews brain cells, and improves muscle injuries.

With all these miracles, it seems as if garlic is a true panacea, but read on.

The Science of Medicine

Separating proven fact from fiction or folklore is a complicated task. There are true believers who tell their stories of cures for diseases with great conviction. Anecdotal evidence is totally convincing to the person who feels better or becomes symptom free. But actual results may be attributable to a variety of causes, and it is the job of science to identify the reasons for any findings.

The first thing I learned in statistics class is that even if two events occur together, one doesn't necessarily cause the other. To illustrate this dictum, my professor cited the high correlation between an increase in the stork popula-

RIGHT TO LEFT: Leek, scallions, and ramps, though considered less potent than garlic, feature in many folk remedies for common ailments.

tion in Holland and an increase in the human birth rate—amusing but true—in the late nineteenth century. As we analyzed the data, we found that as the human population increased, more houses were built. Since storks nested in the chimneys, there was a concomitant increase in the stork population. Although the increase in babies and the increase in storks were tied together, the class couldn't demonstrate that storks brought the babies.

Similarly, people who normally eat lots of garlic may be different from those who eat no garlic in many other respects as well. For example, they may also ingest more olive oil, which is known to be associated with lower blood cholesterol. Or they may eat a more varied diet, a more healthful diet, or fewer prepared foods. So some factor other than garlic eating may be responsible for an observed change.

Random Assignment

Scientific studies in medicine aspire to randomly assign patients to either an experimental group or a control group. The former group is given the drug (or other substance) to be studied, and the latter is given an inert compound, called a placebo. People can't choose which group they will be in, and the study director doesn't choose either. A table of random numbers determines who will be in which group. Random assignment is an easy criterion to meet in garlic studies and must be adhered to if results are to be taken seriously.

Controlled Testing

Ideally, neither the subject in the experiment nor the person checking the results (for example, blood pressure, cholesterol, or bacterial counts) knows whether the subject is in the control group or the experimental group. That way, the experimenter can't bias the results. With garlic studies, controlled testing is extremely difficult. Subjects almost always know whether they're taking garlic, even in powdered pill form, and a researcher with a good nose can almost always tell whether a person has taken garlic or the placebo, because the aroma tends to exude through the skin, no matter what the ads for the products say. Three of the 45 studies mentioned below used a placebo with a garlic odor but no allicins.

Because of the need to control the dosage of allicin, the active ingredient in garlic, fresh garlic has rarely been studied in controlled trials. Yet fresh garlic may very well contain some elements that are lost in processing and thus be more powerful than processed garlic.

Confounding the results in controlled studies is something called the placebo effect. For example, in drug tests, 30 to 35 percent of people in the control group show decided improvement, even though they received the placebo.

Garlic and the Scientific Method

A survey of all the medical studies on the efficacy of garlic was performed in 2000 (Lawrence et al.) for the Agency of Health Care Research of the U.S. Department of Health and Human Services. In a 64-page monograph, the authors reported the results of data analyses from 45 random, controlled tests that lasted at least four weeks. Trials came from Germany (13), North America (14), and India (5), as well as Thailand, Poland, Switzerland, Italy, and Australia. Twenty-two of the studies used dehydrated garlic preparations such as Kwai. Others used oil extracts, cold-pressed garlic oil, or steam-distilled garlic; only two used fresh or fried garlic.

The authors reached the following conclusions:

1. There was a consistent but small decrease in lipids, fats that circulate in the bloodstream; the best known is cholesterol. High levels of lipids have been linked to narrowing of the arteries, which can lead to heart attack and stroke. The effects of garlic are short term. After six months, there are no significant reductions in cholesterol. The greatest benefit is for men with an initial cholesterol reading in the 250 to 300 range. Even the average 12 percent reduction leaves the cholesterol still clinically high.

2. Results on hypertension in adults were mixed. Even in studies that found positive effects, the changes were not large. The studies had many flaws, and the results were unclear.

3. Two studies on insulin sensitivity in adults showed no significant effects of garlic. Twelve small, short-term studies showed that garlic has no significant effect on glucose levels.

4. Ten studies showed "promising" effects of garlic on platelet aggregation, which is a first step in blood clotting. Garlic may reduce thrombosis or blood clots to the heart. But because of "few participants, short follow-

ups, unclear randomization," and other factors, "no firm conclusions can be made" (p. 60).

5. Scant data "suggest but do not prove" that garlic ingestion may be related to a decreased incidence of cancers of the larynx, stomach, colon, rectum, and endometrium, as well as a decrease in the occurrence of colorectal polyps. An ongoing, large-scale study in China may produce more valid results on garlic and precancerous lesions. For other cancers, garlic showed no effects.

6. The most serious adverse effect of garlic was gastrointestinal bleeding. It's unclear whether the bleeding is caused by individual sensitivities, particular preparations, or the way garlic is consumed—ingested, inhaled, or absorbed through the skin. Bleeding may be related to conclusion (4) above, prevention of platelet aggregation. In those who take aspirin regularly to help prevent heart attack or stoke, there is an implication that garlic added to the aspirin may be too much. The same warning goes for drugs commonly known as blood thinners, such as Coumadin or warfarin, heparin, and Trental. Patients taking such drugs should check with their doctors before adding regular doses of garlic to their diets.

Dosage and Side Effects

Experts differ greatly with regard to the effective dosage of garlic. The most common recommendation for fresh garlic is one or two cloves a day, but I've seen some for up to five or even ten cloves a day. Because there are great differences in clove size and strength of active ingredients, both when the garlic is fresh and after it has been stored for six months, results with fresh garlic are very hard to standardize. There is also disagreement on cooking's effect on the potency of the medicinal benefit. Some of the active compounds in garlic are known to increase with cooking, some to decrease. It's impossible to get a reliable answer to this question.

Recommendations differ with regard to processed forms of garlic as well. Enterically coated pills may produce fewer side effects because they are designed to dissolve slowly in the intestines rather than in the stomach. The amount of active ingredients in pills can be as much as 18 times higher in some than in others.

Garlic is also processed in oil and is sometimes steam distilled. There are no reliable studies comparing these forms.

Although one to five cloves of garlic a day is thought to be a safe dose, more is not necessarily better. Even heavenly foods like ripe, fresh tomatoes can cause rashes and gastrointestinal bleeding if you gorge on them in the first flush of summer ripeness. Too much garlic can produce flatulence, nausea, and heartburn. Some experts suggest that garlic in combination with ginkgo and high doses of vitamin E may produce bleeding. There is anecdotal evidence that garlic produces migraine headaches in those who are prone to them, and fresh garlic rubbed on the skin can cause blistering and skin burns. Garlic in fresh or pill form may reduce the effectiveness of HIV drugs.

Rather than chewing a clove of garlic, mince it and add it to milk, juice, yogurt, or applesauce. It is thought that if the garlic isn't chewed, it won't cause odor problems.

Diagnosis

The Hippocratic oath sworn to by all American physicians at graduation is "first, do no harm," and that is a good practice for non-physicians as well. Accurate diagnosis is one of the most critical aspects of treatment. Without the correct diagnosis, relief or cure is almost impossible. Diagnosing oneself is frowned on, among even the most skilled diagnosticians. With self-diagnosis, the probability of bias creeps into the equation. It may be the bias of denial or the opposite and equally dangerous bias of alarmism, the bias of experience and training or the lack thereof.

So for all those who want to dose themselves with herbals, qualified medical care is the first step. From then on, any self-treatment should be reported to your doctor, no matter how embarrassing that confession might be.

CHAPTER FOUR

Alliums in the Garden

Garlic, onions, and leeks are almost always grown for their useful proper-ties—food, flavoring, or health—and the giant alliums are grown pri-marily for their architectural presence in a flower bed. Some of the smaller alliums, such as chives, garlic chives, silver corkscrew chives, and nodding onion, are planted as both culinary and decorative plants. The artificial sepa-ration between culinary and decorative alliums used in chapter 1 can't be per-petuated here as we look at the place of allium in the garden.

Ever since reading Barbara Damrosch's book *Theme Gardens,* I have been fascinated by the idea of using themes in gardens, above and beyond the actual design. I've planted gardens of annuals and perennials whose flowers and leaves could be dried and preserved for everlasting bouquets. To do research for my last book, *Lemon Herbs,* I planted a lemon garden with lemon-flavored herbs such as lemon thyme, lemon-scented geranium, lemon verbena, and lemon southernwood, along with yellow-petaled blooms such as sunflowers and nas-turtiums. I also designed and planted a biblical garden using plants mentioned in the Old Testament at the Jewish Museum of Eastern Pennsylvania.

For some gardeners, the theme is a restricted color palette. They prefer all pastels or all saturated colors, and somehow, each of their gardens winds up looking similar. For others, planting with children in mind means selecting fast-growing, good-tasting, interesting or even scary-looking plants. Many people start with an organizational underpinning that dissipates over the

LEFT: *A.* 'White Giant' glistening with dame's rocket at Wave Hill's Wild Garden.

A. 'Purple Sensation' lives up to its name when paired with a pink or purple clematis, as here in Riverside Park in New York City.

A color-themed bed at the Conservatory Garden in Central Park. *A.* 'Purple Sensation' in back, stars of Persia (*A. christophii*) in front, mixed with blue cat mint, iris, and purple sage—a beautiful sight in late spring.

years as plants die and others fill in to replace them. Species from the original design get interplanted with other favorites, and the plan evolves into something quite different.

Here are some ideas for theme gardens that include allium plants in all their glory.

Butterfly Gardens

Planting to attract butterflies means knowing which butterflies live in or migrate to your area and adding host plants on which butterflies lay their eggs and caterpillars feed and nectar plants that attract the adults. Many species gravitate to wildflowers, especially daisies, milkweed, goldenrod, joe-pye weed, black-eyed Susan, asters, Queen Anne's lace, and nettles. After all, butterflies were laying eggs, developing caterpillars, and collecting nectar long before humans first cultivated flower gardens for their own delight. In our carefully tended gardens, we yearn for butterflies to appear near the patio or porch where we can best admire them. In addition to favored plants such as lantana *(Lantana camara),* butterfly bush *(Buddleia* spp.), coreopsis *(Coreopsis* spp.), and blazing star *(Liatris* spp.), chives and other early alliums are often recommended to fill in the early flowering cycle. Butterfly plants should vary in height to attract species that prefer flying at different levels, and a selection of plants should bloom throughout the growing season. Chives are among the early bloomers with low-growing flowers that smaller species may prefer. Garlic chives attract monarchs, painted ladies, and swallowtails. Focus on fragrance as a characteristic attractant, and plant Naples garlic *(Allium neapolitanum)* for that purpose. A water source, even a tin of water on the ground, is also a lure.

If you are trying to attract butterflies, bear in mind the importance of organic methods of gardening. Pesticide use in any area of the garden, including the lawn, can be dangerous to their health.

Gardens for Everlasting Bouquets

You'll be the most popular person on your block if you grow enough dried material to distribute to neighbors or donate to decorate the local library, church, or historic home.

Plant easy annuals such as cockscomb *(Celosia cristata),* larkspur *(Consolida ambigua),* love-in-a-mist *(Nigella damascena),* and straw flowers *(Helichrysum bracteatum),* all of which can be dried by hanging them in bunches in a warm, dark, dry spot. Plant hardy perennials such as lamb's ears *(Stachys byzantina),* yarrow *(Achillea* spp.), globe thistle *(Echinops ritro),* deep red peonies *(Paeonia),* and tansy *(Tanacetum)* for long-lived beauty. Among the alliums, include chives and drumstick allium *(A. sphaerocephalon)* for the flowers and garlic chives *(A. tuberosum)* and stars of Persia *(A. christophii)* for both small and giant seed heads. If you have room, incorporate at least one or two peegee hydrangea *(H. paniculata* 'Grandiflora') to provide the mass that pulls everything together.

See my book *Flower Crafts* for a comprehensive list of almost 100 garden plants and wildflowers that dry well and look beautiful in arrangements, as well as when and how to harvest and dry them and create arrangements. See chapter 6 for instructions on drying allium.

Spires and Spheres

Imagine an enchanted city with dramatic spires and spheres—delicate in aroma, strong in color—a place for fairies and elves to hide. This is a garden that blooms brightest in late spring. It is based on architecture, form, and style and can be backed up by shrubbery to great effect. My preference in shrubs is boxwood, sheared into pyramids or inverted cones, or pyramidal juniper, which requires only the slightest pruning to keep it in shape.

Select some of your favorite spired perennials such as delphinium, foxglove, and lupines. One of the cultivated mulleins is another possibility. These all have multiple flowers along tall stems; certain varieties of delphiniums can reach 5 feet.

Pair these spires with the spheres of flowering onions. This is an opportunity to use large-headed alliums and have them seem in perfect scale. Select from *A. giganteum,* 'Globemaster', 'Lucy Ball', or 'Gladiator' for a big sphere that stands above the crowd. Plant stars of Persia *(A. christophii)* or Turkestan onion *(A. karataviense)* for low-growing but still large-headed flower balls. Fill in with larkspur, for its spikes, and love-in-a-mist, which has puffs of delicate flowers followed by ball- or egg-shaped striped seed pods that are perfect for drying. Both these annuals reseed themselves for years if you harvest no more than half the flowers or pods.

The drama of this garden depends on simultaneous blooming, like a drawing in a garden catalog. But the allium seed heads provide the shapely structure of their spheres even after all the petals have fallen.

An informal grouping of contrasting spires and spheres in the Wild Garden at Wave Hill.

Rock and Alpine Gardens

Rock and alpine gardens usually consist of perennials with all shades of foliage—yellows, blues, and gray-greens—and all forms of plants—matting, clumping, tufting, trailing, cushions, and rosettes. These plants are particularly suited to shallow, rocky soil, and many are hardy enough to survive high altitudes and nearly constant snow. If the location is south facing, that is ideal.

Flowering alliums prefer well-drained soil in a sunny location, and the small species are ideally suited to most rock gardens. Although alliums like a soil rich in organic matter, they are planted more shallowly than most bulbs—only an inch deep for the smaller ones. Therefore, digging in rocky soil is not an issue. There are many colors to choose from, including white, yellow, pink, lavender, and purple, and even a range of shapes, from tight balls to graceful pendants of drooping bells. The smaller the species, the more interesting they look close up, either in standard beds or on ledges or platforms with containers.

Frelinghuysen Arboretum in Morris County, New Jersey, has a large and interesting raised alpine display complete with appropriate rocks and interesting species, including silver corkscrew chives (*Allium senescens glaucum*). Everything is nicely labeled to assist the home gardener in making choices. Other species appropriate for rock gardens and alpine displays are listed in the accompanying table. The same plants can be used for miniature villages and garden model train layouts.

ALLIUM SPECIES FOR ALPINE AND ROCK GARDENS

Species	Common Name	Height (inches)	Color
A. cernuum	Nodding onion	12–16	Light pink to magenta
A. karataviense	Turkestan onion	8–10	White to pale pink
A. moly	Lily leek	10–18	Yellow
A. neapolitanum	Naples garlic	12–20	White
A. oreophylum	—	10	Purple
A. roseum	Rosy flowered garlic	10–15	White to pale pink
A. senescens glaucum	Curly chives	6–8	Pale pink to lavender
A. unifolium	—	12	Pink

Heirloom Gardens

Those who own historic homes often plan their gardens in keeping with the vintage of the structure. Designers of gardens for museums and public historic homes have even more reason to ensure that the plants they choose reflect the period of the building. The Strawbery Banke Museum in Portsmouth, New Hampshire, has an even more complicated mission. The museum relocates local buildings from various eras and preserves them on 10 acres along the Piscataqua River. Because the buildings were once homes, barns, artisan workshops, and stores that date from the 1690s to 1950s, the garden designers have quite a job choosing plantings that harmonize with the era of each structure. For example, a victory garden is planted near the 1940s grocery store; a backyard kitchen garden and orchard are planted behind a 1720s home. Many of the gardens include culinary or flowering alliums.

Allium species are readily available to fit most of the periods in U.S. gardens. They are perennial, require little care, and are easy to interplant among other annuals and perennials. Companion annuals that have a wonderful old-time appearance and evoke memories of Grandma's garden are the tall and long-blooming spider flower *(Cleome hasslerana)* and the self-sowing annual lark-

Strawbery Banke Museum matches the era of each of its many buildings with an heirloom garden from the same era. PHOTO FROM STRAWBERY BANKE MUSEUM

The Victory garden, a form of planting popular in the 1940s, at Strawbery Banke, with onions almost ready to pull, carrots, beets, and dill.

spur *(Consolida ambigua).* The highly fragrant but tender perennial heliotrope *(Heliotropium arborescens)* can be grown as an annual. Flowering tobacco *(Nicotiana alata),* true-blue bachelor's button *(Centaurea cyanus),* biennial sweet William *(Dianthus barbatus),* and tall hollyhocks *(Alcea rosea)* are also appropriate in a historic American garden, brought over with the colonists. Some favorite perennials for an heirloom flower garden are bleeding hearts, phlox, yarrow, peonies, and poppies. No heirloom garden would be complete without one of the antique roses, which are highly fragrant but usually have a brief bloom time. Look for one that is disease resistant.

Before planting an heirloom garden, it's fun to take a trip to a historic site to view the gardens and gain both inspiration and tips. Colonial Williamsburg in Virginia; Shaker villages in Massachusetts, New Hampshire, and Kentucky; Bartram's Gardens in Philadelphia; Thomas Jefferson's home, Monticello, in Virginia; and the Missions in California offer interesting insights into what period gardens might have looked like.

Some gardens at historic sites have been prettified to please the modern eye, so do a little sleuthing into their authenticity before you make the trip. Another caveat: Just because a species is an heirloom, many of the modern cultivars are anything but. Those double and triple powder-puff hollyhocks sold in garden centers today are a far cry from the single-flowered *Alcea* species brought from England by settlers in the 1600s. Read labels carefully, ask a horticulturist, and consider ordering seeds or plants from one of the heirloom seed companies. Catalogs such as Scheepers, Brent and Becky's Bulbs, and White Flower Farm specify the heirloom varieties they sell. (see sources on page 143).

In addition to the flowering onions, many of the old varieties of edible garlic, onions, chives, leeks, Egyptian onions, and shallots can be included in a historic vegetable or herb garden. Sarah Wolfgang Heffner suggests the onions 'Red Wethersfield' (also a favorite of the horticulturist at Hancock Shaker Village in Massachusetts), 'Southport White Globe', 'White Portugal', and 'Early Yellow Globe'.

Biblical Gardens

Biblical gardens consist of plants mentioned in the Bible, and they usually include labels and booklets that describe the uses of each plant in ancient times and the quotation to which it refers. There are many biblical gardens in the United States, including those in New York City; Providence, Rhode Island; Coral Gables, Florida; Pittsburgh, Pennsylvania; Charleston, South Carolina; and Carmel and Camarillo, California.

As recorded in the Book of Exodus, Moses led his people away from Egypt, where they had been enslaved by the Pharaoh, and into the wilderness, but they didn't find the food they craved. In Numbers 11:5, the people cried out, saying, "We remember the fish which we did eat in Egypt freely, the cucumbers and the melons and the leeks and the onions and the garlic." I planted onions, leeks, chives and garlic chives, to illustrate this passage.

When I designed a biblical garden for the Jewish Museum of Eastern Pennsylvania, I included only Old Testament plants. Some of those mentioned as food plants in the Bible, in addition to the alliums, were dates and figs, almonds, grapes for wine, wheat and barley, lettuce, lentils, and olives. Of course, the fruit of the tree of life was also mentioned, but not by name. Although paintings in the Western tradition often depict Adam and Eve under an apple tree, apples were probably not native to the Holy Land. I included fig, quince, and apricot, which are more likely candidates.

The garden produces flax, which was spun and woven into linen for the priests, and herbs such as thyme, sage, bay, laurel, coriander, chamomile, dan-

HEIRLOOM FLOWERING ALLIUMS AND APPROXIMATE DATE OF INTRODUCTION

Species	Date
A. caeruleum	1792
A. carniatum pulchellum	1810
A. cernuum	1798
A. flavum	1759
A. karataviense	1876
A. rosenbachianum	1884
A. roseum	1753
A. schubertii	1843
A. sphaerocephalon	1594
A. triquetrum	1789
A. unifolium	1873

The Rodef Shalom Biblical Botanical Garden in Pittsburgh includes hundreds of plants mentioned in the Old Testament. Allium and water plants are prominently displayed.

Chinese chives ready to bloom in the Biblical Garden of Eastern Pennsylvania in Pottsville.

delion, lemon grass, and parsley, which were used medicinally, to preserve food, and for flavoring. Certain plants that won't grow in horticultural zone 5.5 are represented in an indoor display—cotton, cinnamon, pomegranate, and palm, to name a few. It's a project of interest to historians, to gardeners, to children and adults studying the Bible, and to neighbors who would just like to sit in a peaceful garden and contemplate this verse from Isaiah 55:12–13:

> For ye shall go out with joy and be led forth with peace;
> The mountains and the hills shall break forth before you with singing,
> And all the trees of the field shall clap their hands.
> Instead of the thorn shall come up the cypress
> And instead of the briar shall come up the myrtle.

For further information, see *Plants of the Bible* by Harold and Alma Moldenke.

Leeks are permitted to flower in the Biblical Garden. The stone cistern, now dry, illustrates the importance of water to a desert people.

Children's Gardens

Every children's garden must contain several of the giant alliums. Children will see humor in *A. giganteum* 'Gladiator' or 'Globemaster'. The resemblance to a lollipop or a balloon is unmistakable, as is the plant's need to rise above many others in the garden. Certainly include the shorter sunflowers, such as 'Elf' or 'Teddy Bear', and the mammoth varieties, such as 'Russian Giant'. Have a miniature pumpkin ('Jack-Be-Little') and a giant pumpkin vine, as well as shaped gourds that can be dried and used in crafts.

Include cherry tomatoes for their flavor. If your child is still in the rigid stage, skip the flavorful but startlingly yellow 'Sun Gold' and substitute the properly red 'Sweet 100' or 'Sweet 1 Million'. Plant lamb's ears for the texture (and for the tales that before Charmin it was used as toilet paper, and before Band-Aids it was used for cuts and scrapes). Don't forget strawflowers to show that something growing can still feel all dried out. Children also love Japanese lanterns for their shape and color, although the roots can spread outrageously. Plant pansies for their resemblance to little faces and snapdragons so that you can demonstrate how to make the mouth snap open.

A secret place in the center or at the edge of the garden is always a treat. Hideouts can be made from simple tented trellises with rapidly growing vines such as morning glory or scarlet runner beans trained on them. Podded peas are a useful substitute. One of my daughter's six-year-old friends couldn't believe that peas grow in "such neat little packages," having previously seen only Birds Eye frozen. Giant sunflowers planted in a small patch provide a natural hideout among the leaves and stalks.

Herb Gardens

Formal

A formal herb garden is built on a geometric plan and often repeats the shapes of beds and even specific plants in a well-ordered design. The plan is often four squares or rectangles with paths between them and a focal point

An exquisite formal herb garden framed by gray santolina at Government House, Victoria, British Columbia. Chives are a small part of the garden, which features lots of sage, thyme, and lavender.

such as a fountain, statue, sundial, or birdbath in the center. Plans can get more complicated with multiple blocks of squares, a circle in a square, or a square in a circle, each repeated. Triangles or diamonds may intersperse with other geometric forms. The more complicated designs are usually reserved for public gardens with staffs of gardeners to keep everything in order. A simple plan for the home gardener might be a circle divided into quarters or eighths. For a restricted space, a wagon wheel can be laid flat with plants massed between the spokes.

A heart-stopping garden at Chateau Villandry, in France's Loire Valley, takes the formal herb garden plan to the limit. It has fruit trees, vegetables, and all manner of edibles, including onions and leeks, both in natural form and shaped into topiaries, espaliers, and trellises, with walking paths throughout. This is one of my all-time favorite gardens.

Knot gardens are prized by formal herb gardeners as well. Form and structure are essential. Plants appear to weave in and out among one another and must grow in well-ordered clumps, as do many of the alliums.

Smaller alliums lend themselves to formal herb gardens, appropriate in rows in front of the border. Look for varieties that keep their leaves and don't

In late September, the chives which border this herb bed are still in full foliage at Frelinghuysen Arboretum in Morris County, New Jersey.

enter into summer dormancy. My favorites for herb gardens are chives and silver corkscrew chives because they are short, and the foliage remains until the first frost. Many pot herbs have unremarkable flowers, so either of these chive species provides a riot of color by comparison, albeit a pastel pink or mauve.

Consider both flower and foliage color, as well as height, when selecting combinations for the herb garden. Listed below are some plants that are particularly attractive in combination with small alliums.

- Purple-leaved basils such as *Ocimum basilicum* 'Purple Ruffles' or 'Dark Opal' or *Perilla frutescens* 'Atropurpurea'.

- Silver-leaved herbs such as 'Silver King' (*Artemisia ludoviciana* var. *albula*) or lavender cotton (*Santolina chamaecyparissus*).

- One of the hardy lavenders, such as *Lavandula angustifolia* 'Lady' or 'Hidcote', or one of the tender lavenders, especially *L. stoechus* (sometimes called Spanish lavender).

- Heliotrope (*Heliotropium arborescens*), with its vivid purple flowers, and blue salvia (*Salvia farinacea* 'Victoria'), with its short spikes of intense blue, grow as annuals in colder areas. Plant them in spring when chives are deep into their bloom time. Silver corkscrew chives bloom in mid to late summer, when these annuals will be in fine fettle.

- Other perennial herbs to combine with alliums are blue-flowering cat mint (*Nepeta*) and purple-leaved culinary sage (*Salvia officinalis* 'Purpurascens').

Purple basil and allium seed head are a winning combination.

Egyptian onion, calendula, borage, and thyme in a backyard kitchen garden from a c. 1720 design at Strawbery Banke Museum.

Informal

Those who lack the time, the patience, or the inclination to plant a formal, well-ordered, highly structured herb garden can have the same combinations of plants with much less work. Whether the herbs are grown in one container, mixed into a perennial border, planted among the vegetables, or under-planted among the hybrid roses, those who want fresh herbs will find a way—if only on a windowsill, balcony, ledge, or fire escape.

Go to a community garden anywhere in the United States and peer into the small allotments offered to neighborhood gardeners. Alliums are well represented among the plant selections, regardless of the ethnic background of the neighborhood, with garlic, onion, and chives predominating.

Herbal Themes

Some herb gardens tackle more specific themes, such as culinary or medicinal herbs. There are sensory gardens highlighting fragrant and tactile herbs, sometimes planted for the visually impaired; gardens for dye plants; good gardens from historical periods such as the Middle Ages or colonial American. Alliums have their place in each of these gardens.

Leeks at the Cloisters Museum in New York City.

Medieval gardens usually combine food, flavoring, medicinal, and dye plants; garlic, onions, and leeks are included on all counts. The Cloisters Museum, part of the Metropolitan Museum of Art in New York City, has three medieval gardens that complement the famous art and architecture collections. Included are plants such as lavender, false indigo, lady's bedstraw, bear's breeches, and about 250 other species cultivated in the Middle Ages. Leeks are as showy as any flower there, though they were grown historically as edibles, not to show off.

Alliums for Shade and Partial Shade

In the never-ending search for colorful shade plants, several alliums come to mind. In many horticultural zones, seven alliums may solve some problems. Try *A. karataviense,* with its colorful leaves as well as flowers; *A. moly* for dry shade; *A. senescens* for late summer blooms; *A. thunbergii* for a last burst of bloom in late fall; *A. triquetrum,* which naturalizes in shade; *A. unifolium,* which tolerates moist soil; and *A. zebdanense,* an early bloomer.

A. moly 'Jeannine' welcomes dry shade.

LEFT: Darlene and Don Huntington understand that an allium seed head is as important as an allium in full flower. RIGHT: Allium seed heads set off by goldenrod and
gay feather in mid-August near Seattle.

Mixed Borders

The mixed border is often an excellent site for your favorite alliums. For
species whose foliage yellows or becomes dormant, it's a good idea to have the
plant happily ensconced among others. The giant alliums look especially
appropriate in a long bed of mixed herbacious perennials, shrubs, and other

larger elements. The short alliums that retain their leaves, such as chives, are excellent for the front of the border, because both the foliage and the flowers are long lasting. In addition, chives are one of the first perennials to bloom in spring, right after (or sometimes with) spring bulbs.

Deer-Resistant Gardens

Gardening in deer country is a topic worthy of its own literature. Suffice it to say that Vincent Drzewucki Jr., author of *Gardening in Deer Country,* gives the giant alliums his highest rating for resistance to deer. Reports from other gardeners all over the country indicate that other *Allium* species are also shunned by deer and many other animals. Plant alliums with lavender, hostas, bee balm, yarrow, monkshood, and many of the culinary and fragrant herbs for a deer-resistant garden.

The Wild Garden at Wave Hill, not to be confused with a native wild flower garden, is a mass of bloom through much of the year in the Bronx.

Container Gardens

Kitchen Herbs

When you have a small garden or only a small patch of sun around your house, or perhaps only a windowsill or a fire escape, think container herb gardening. For most culinary purposes, only small amounts of fresh herbs are needed to flavor the pot. And it's so handy to have them near the kitchen, even if you have several acres for planting, as I used to. Sloth rears its ugly head when I have to walk 300 yards to cut a little rosemary to sprinkle on the lamb steak for dinner, and I'd rather forgo the chopped chives on the scrambled eggs if it means getting my slippers wet with dew.

Containers are the perfect solution, and the best alliums for a mixed container are fairly small ones such as chives *(A. schoenoprasum)*, silver corkscrew chives, and garlic chives. They will all be perennial in a large enough pot. The ubiquitous half whiskey barrels are useful containers for planting mixed herbs outdoors. Set the container in full sun, make sure there is excellent drainage, and water when the soil is dry. Combine any of these alliums with one plant of purple sage *(Salvia officinalis* 'Purpurascens'), purple basil *(Ocimum basilicum purpurescens)*, lemon thyme, dill, parsley *(Pet-*

Peppers, chives, and chamomile in a planter at Epcot Center, Florida.

roselinum crispum), or prostrate rosemary for the edges of the pot. The sage and thyme are winter-hardy herbacious perennials. Parsley is a biennial that is best the first year started from seed. You may have to replant others yearly, depending on your horticultural zone.

If you're working with only pots on the windowsill, common chives are one of the most long lasting. Chive leaves, buds, and flowers are all tasty. The

Jane and Bill Fowler constructed raised beds on top of an old tennis court for their fabulous collection of ornamentals, edibles, and old objects.

Another Epcot planter, this one featuring purple basil, chives, and kale.

plants actually benefit from getting a haircut as you trim the tops to season your cooking. They will grow into clumps about 6 inches wide and 6 to 9 inches high, but they may never bloom if you keep up the trimming. Indoor chives won't keep growing unless they are given a rest period out in the garden, but you can always get a few new bulbs from a friend and start over. You will be treated with fresh herbs during the winter months.

Containers with Mixed Ornamentals

Because alliums are planted shallowly and because the foliage often dies back and goes completely dormant, they lend themselves to the crowded conditions in most containers. Any of the alliums will grow, provided the drainage is excellent and there is plenty of sun. One fan even suggests planting giant allium in a container, but that's where I draw the line.

CHAPTER FIVE

Growing Alliums

Alliums can be planted from bulbs; from divisions of larger perennial plants; from sets, or immature plants; from small corms that form at the base of bulbs; from bulbils; and from seeds. Flowering alliums are usually planted from bulbs, which you can purchase from many reliable sources (see page 143). Reject those that appear nicked, slashed, or shriveled. Some plants will drop seed and volunteer in the garden. Like other members of the lily family (Liliaceae), older bulbs can be divided to make more. Some develop small corms or cormels at the base that can be dug and replanted. The corms are encased in a hard shell that should be soaked for two to three days before planting. Eventually, they will bloom.

Buy chives, garlic chives, and corkscrew chives as small plants from garden centers, plant them from seeds, or get divisions from other gardeners who are ready to dig and divide. Some species such as garlic and leeks take two to three years to mature. Buying sets allows you to bring the crop to harvest the same year you plant. Some varieties are sterile, so you will need to get divisions from friends or buy them in pots.

LEFT: Leaving the seed head to develop in the garden after the flower blooms results in a second spectacular show.

In the Garden

Chives

Allium schoenoprasum

Chives can be planted in full sun or partial shade. They grow in clumps of thin, elongated bulbs that form off rhizomes. Chives can be grown easily from seeds, which allows you a choice of varieties. Every garden center that sells herbs includes chives in its array.

Clumps can be dug and divided every few years for a never-ending supply, and they readily self-sow in the garden. Save a few divisions for a winter windowsill herb garden.

Garlic Chives

Allium tuberosum

Garlic chives prefer full sun but can also tolerate partial shade. They can be grown from divisions. If you buy them in pots or sow seeds, they will produce flowers in 60 to 90 days. Divide clumps every three to four years. If you don't pick the flowers, garlic chives will be prolific reseeders. This plant looks good among chive flowers, which bloom earlier. The white flowers are a nice addition to the late summer herb garden, and the seed pods are attractive in the fall and winter garden.

Onions

Allium cepa

The most common onion is the globe onion, which forms large, edible bulbs underground. Onions have hollow stems and leaves. Although the typical home gardener harvests onions the same year they're planted from sets outdoors or started from seeds early in the season indoors, onions are actually biennial. The designation

'Super Star' onion, an All-American selections winner with a mild, sweet flavor at the Burpee trial gardens. This onion is day-length neutral, meaning it grows well in both northern and southern climes.

comes from the fact that it takes two seasons for the plants to go through their entire growing cycle, flower, and set seeds. Home gardeners typically don't want onion flowers and don't save the seeds, so the process of growing for eating can be accomplished in one season. The flowers, however, are excellent for dried arrangements.

FROM SEEDS

When starting seeds in a soilless mix indoors, cover them very lightly and keep the mix barely moist. Before planting time, trim the grasslike tops to about 3 inches, and sprinkle the cuttings on soups, salads, and vegetables, as you would chives.

If you save your own seeds from year to year, you should keep the purity of the strain by not crossbreeding. Recommendations to prevent crossbreeding vary from 100 feet to 1 mile separation between varieties. Wait to harvest the seeds until they are visible on the flowers; then pick the flowers, hang them to dry, and shake the seeds into a paper bag.

FROM SETS

Plant onion sets outdoors when the soil temperature is about 40 degrees. Plant them with the pointed end up, root end down, about 1 inch deep. St. Patrick's Day is the signal in northeastern Pennsylvania to start planting onions. Any late snowfall is dubbed "the onion snow"—one that won't stay long on the ground, and a reminder that you must get busy planting.

Onions need sun; excellent drainage; and moderately fertile, loose, loamy soil, because the roots are short. Adding compost and other organic matter to the soil increases the bulb size. They do poorly in clay soil. Onions need adequate moisture regularly, but the water must be able to run off. Water 1 to 2 inches a week if there is no rain. To encourage large bulb growth, onion sets should be planted close together, then thinned to the desired distance. The thinnings can be eaten like chives or bunching onions.

When you notice the first onion leaves turning yellow in mid to late summer, bend all the leaves in the row down to the ground to hasten ripening for an earlier harvest. Stop watering so the bulbs can dry off as much as possible in the ground. Wait about a week, then pull all the plants at once as the leaves start to turn brown. If you wait too long, the leaves will pull off as you tug on the bulb, and you'll have to dig instead. Allow the onions to cure in the sun on screens. Cover them with a plastic sheet or tarp or bring them indoors each night to avoid dew and rain. Curing time is about two weeks, until the outer skin turns papery. Then the onions can be stored. It pays to examine your onions even after storage and remove any that are starting to get moldy, rot, or sprout. As with apples, one bad onion can spoil the "barrel."

Garlic
Allium sativum
PLANTING FROM CLOVES

Growing garlic from cloves is a form of cloning. Each clove from one head has identical qualities. Start with a nice, unblemished head of garlic and divide it into cloves no more than a day or two before you are ready to plant. The cloves should be very firm; discard any soft ones, as they could spread disease. Pop the cloves from the base by first slitting the papery wrapper with your fingernail, being careful not to bruise the cells at the base of the clove. Each head will yield 3 to 20 cloves. *Do not peel the cloves.* Save the smallest cloves for cooking, and select the biggest as your "seed" stock. Given some time and attention, garlic bulbs will have to be purchased only once. After that, you can save your own stock each year to replant and perform the agriculturist function of customizing your stock to the growing conditions in your garden. By using big cloves from good-sized bulbs each year, you are selecting hardy genetic stock. Thus, two growers who buy from the same source in the same year will have garlic with a slightly different size, taste, and color five years later just by making different selections from their own gardens. If you want to select for color, that is possible too.

There are more than 600 varieties of garlic available in this country alone, many with somewhat strange names. It seems that each farmer who hand-selects and then sells stock to new growers names his or her own garlic. I came across the "Andy Porcelain" at one garlic festival; the original seed stock had been given to the grower by her neighbor Andy, and the grower honored his generosity by naming the variety after him.

The cloves should be planted in the fall: late September to early October in New England; early October to around Columbus Day in Pennsylvania and New York. Garlic prefers to grow sturdy roots in the fall before the ground freezes and then rest over winter before the first green shoots come up in March. The farther south you live, the later you can plant. In warm regions, plant in early winter. A general guideline is to begin planting four to six weeks before the ground usually freezes. You don't want the new shoots to come up before winter. Some northern growers wait and plant in early spring as soon as the ground can be worked, making harvest a few weeks later and usually cutting down on the yield.

Buy garlic for your garden from a reliable grower by mail or at a farm market or garlic festival (see sources). Don't plant garlic purchased at the supermarket; it has usually been treated with a growth inhibitor and will probably disappoint. Pay particular attention to your horticultural growing zone, and know what zone the cloves came from. A good match between the mother bulb's zone and the zone of your garden will give you a good head start.

Garlic needs full sun, lots of water, and soil with excellent drainage. It prefers rich soil with lots of organic matter mixed in, so add well-rotted manure or compost to the soil well in advance of planting. Bulbs may become misshapen in heavy clay soil or with too little water. In years when there is little snowfall or rain, smaller or misshapen bulbs may result.

Plant in rows, with the cloves set 6 inches apart and at a depth of 2 to 4 inches. In a mild area, planting 1 inch deep will work. The rows

Buying garlic or swapping information at the Pocona Garlic Festival in Stroudsburg, Pennsylvania.

should be at least 12 inches apart to give the bulbs adequate growing room and to give you adequate room to weed and cultivate. Set the clove with the fat side down and the tip up. Farmers who plant mechanically don't bother with this nicety and find that the clove knows what it's doing. With winter heaves caused by frost, most of the cloves right themselves by springtime and know which way is up. I prefer to help my cloves along by giving them the best possible start in life.

Mulch rows with chopped leaves, grass cuttings (without weed killer), or straw. Mulch helps keep the weeds down and the soil moist. It works its way into the soil as it decomposes. Mulching also helps keep the soil cooler in the South, where that is needed. Having said this, some growers send instructions with their bulbs in capital letters, "DO NOT MULCH." Why? Mulch can contain weed seeds, necessitating more weeding chores. Or if the mulch is too compact, it can actually keep water from the plants. However, the needs of commercial garlic growers and home gardeners are different, so experiment and find the method that works best for you in your locale. My own method is to mulch heavily between the rows, generally keeping the mulch about 6 inches from the base of the plants. That way, the amount of weeding is minimized. I prefer hand weeding, which gets me down on my knees in close communion with the plants, where I'm alerted to changes in growth patterns or problems, which I wouldn't see standing up wielding a hoe.

Fertilize with kelp or fish emulsion about three times, starting when you see the leaves pop up in spring until about two months before harvest. Northerners will fertilize for the last time in the middle of May for a mid-July harvest. Pull weeds to cut down on competition and to grow bigger bulbs. Garlic hates competition from other plants, whether weeds or desirables.

If you have a top-setting garlic that makes a coil on the scape, the shoot should be cut off after the coil appears to prevent bulbils from forming. This happens in late May or early June. That way, all the energy is going into the bulb. If you want bulbils for future plantings, let a small part of the crop grow into the capsule, then cut the capsules as soon as they mature in late June or early July. I save some of the stalks with bulbs attached to dry for flower arrangements (see chapter 6). Some growers use the fresh scapes or top-sets in salads, stir-fries, and sautés.

By the middle of June, the cycle is winding down, and the bulbs are usually pulled in mid to late July. But in Texas, for example, the whole cycle is accelerated, and the crop can be ready to harvest in early to mid-May. When the first leaves start to yellow, stop all watering. The sign to harvest garlic is when the first leaves in the row yellow and fall over. Home gardeners harvest by pulling up on the stems at the base of the plant. Pull a test plant to make sure that the size is adequate and the bulb is well formed. Some growers say to pull plants when 60 percent of the leaves have yellowed; some say when five or six leaves are still green or when the stalks are one-third to one-half brown. If left in the ground too long, the cloves will start to separate from the main head and split apart, leading to in-ground disease, rot, or poor storage quality when dug.

GROWING GARLIC FROM BULBILS

Most farmers of top-setting (hard-neck) garlic allow some of their plants to grow capsules and then save the tiny bulbils inside. They're about the size of a grain of wheat and are not considered true seeds but tiny, aerial bulbs. When cured and replanted, these bulbils will grow into bulbs, but it takes three years or more to reach full size. Plan on a long-term use of the field and lots of labor to weed, water, and fertilize for this three-year period. Bulbils are usually saved in case the entire bulb crop is wiped out in a disastrous year. Having some bulbils planted safe underground, or having some in the shed ready to plant, if necessary, is a form of insurance. If your great-grandmother brought the original 'Rocambole' bulbs from Poland in the 1890s and your family has been planting and saving the stock in each generation, there is every reason to have bulbil insurance.

CURING

After garlic is pulled, it must be cured and cleaned. Home gardeners can afford to baby their crops a little more than farmers who've planted 10,000 bulbs.

Gently brush off most of the dirt clinging to the bulbs. I know some growers who hose off their crops before curing, but most don't. Lay out the garlic, stems and all, on old screens in a dark, dry, cool spot. If you choose to set your screens in the shade of a tree, as some people do, you must be on the lookout for rain the way a laundress is with the sheet hanging on the clothesline, and bring them in right away when a downpour or even a drizzle threatens.

Some growers prefer to bunch and hang garlic to start the curing process. In fact, I've never heard so much individual and conflicting advice about any crop—flower or vegetable—as there is for garlic. One hobby grower I know lets his crop cure on tarps on the ground. He swears that the nightly dew doesn't hurt the crop, but I'm not so sure.

Cure for about two weeks, either hanging in bunches in a warm, dry spot or laid out on screens. Then trim off the roots with small shears or garden scissors. If you don't need the stems for craft work, such as braids or swags, cut off the stems about an inch from the top. The stems should have tightened up around the top of the bulb.

Garlic is cured on screens.

SAVING "SEED"

Sort through and select the best bulbs for your planting or "seed" stock for next season, and set these aside so you won't eat them by accident. Store bulbs in a basket or hanging mesh bag in a cool, airy place. Use several baskets rather than one large one to allow for better airflow. Refrigeration is a poor way of storing, because the humidity is too high and the air circulation too poor. Bulbs have a tendency to mildew in such an environment.

When you're ready to plant, the heads must be carefully broken into individual cloves.

DISEASES AND PESTS

Garlic and onions are susceptible to thrips (sucking insects), nematodes (tiny wormlike creatures that invade the leaves and stems), mites, maggots (which attack stored bulbs), worms, rot, and mold—a rather long list. For the home gardener, familiar methods of garden hygiene can help ward off problems. Start with unblemished stock from a reputable grower. Rotate your crops, planting all alliums (except for the perennials) in new locations on a three-year rotation scheme. Dig infected plants and burn them—don't compost. It's probably best to burn stems, roots, and bulb wrappers that come off healthy plants during harvest as well. Don't plant alliums in low ground, where water will stand, and don't crowd plants in the field. Store bulbs in smallish batches, and remove any that start to rot. Again, don't compost these rejects, or you may be returning problems to your garden next year. For a fine discussion on allium pests and diseases, as well as planting techniques, see *Growing Great Garlic* by Ron L. Engeland.

Leeks
Allium porrum
Buy seeds or sets from catalogs or growers. The sets look like wild chives when they come—a bundle of little green things with tiny bulbs at the bottom. Start seeds indoors in flats eight weeks before the last frost is expected in spring. Set seedlings out in rows about two weeks before the last frost, planting them 6 inches apart in rows 24 inches apart. Some prefer to set the seedlings 1 inch apart and then transplant again to 6 inches apart, but I'd rather save the work of thinning and retransplanting, even if it leaves an occasional hole in a row where one has failed to thrive.

The traditional method is to plant in trenches 8 inches deep and to keep hilling up the soil around the stems as they grow. This keeps the bottom parts white from lack of chlorophyll. It's the tender white part that is used in cooking. Some growers, however, plant in flat beds and use mulch such as grass clippings to hill up the stalks. That method may be a little harder, because the mulch gets quite deep and must be kept in place to be effective.

Gardeners who are growing leeks as an edible crop prefer to cut off the flower stalk and even the tops of the leaves before they mature to force more energy into the roots and stalk. I love to watch the flower open and leave a few stalks in the garden to enjoy the sight, or I bring them indoors as a cut flower.

Pick a few early and use like bunching onions, as the leaves are more tender farther up the stalk.

Leeks can withstand some frost in the fall, making them a wonderful late crop to pull as needed for use in the kitchen. Try hilling up mulch against the stems in fall, and you will probably be able to harvest for most of the winter.

Leeks in bloom at the Heronswood vegetable garden of Dan Hinkley.

Elephant Garlic

Allium ampeloprasum

Purchase bulbs from a reliable source and carefully pull them apart, following the earlier instructions for true garlic. Plant cloves 8 inches apart. The bulbs that form send up flower stalks, which must be cut off to produce bigger bulbs. The bulbs themselves form tiny, hard-shelled corms at their base, which can eventually produce new bulbs. After pulling the elephant garlic for harvest, remove these corms carefully and store them in a cool, dry spot. When you're ready to replant next season, soak the corms in warm water for several days. Like true garlic, elephant garlic takes several years to reach full size from the planting of corms, so be patient. If you can't wait, you can always plant from cloves. Follow other instructions for planting true garlic as well.

Shallots

Allium ascalonicum

Shallots are grown from seeds or bulbs. Planting in the fall is preferred, as with garlic, but either seeds or bulbs can be planted in the spring for a smaller yield. Gardeners in warm climates where the ground doesn't freeze in winter usually plant in January or early February and harvest before the most intense summer heat.

If you're lucky, supermarket purchases will sprout when planted in the garden. Here, some elephant garlic grows among the many unusual plants at Heronwood.

Space the plants 4 to 6 inches apart in rows 18 inches apart. The tops of the bulbs should be 1 to 2 inches below the soil, with the root side down. When bulbing begins, stop fertilizing and watering. The bulbs, if not planted too deeply, will push up to the surface and dry. Harvest when most of the tops are brown, lifting with a fork and then gently pulling by hand. If you wait too long, the shallots are likely to rot from any

A braid of shallots with whiny ambers wrappers makes a beautiful decoration.

rains that come along. Shallots, like garlic and onions, can be injured at this point by careless handling before the wrappers are cured and fully dried. If bruised, they will rot in storage.

Cure shallots for two to three weeks spread out on screens in a cool, dry spot; then trim off the roots and stems with pruning shears, leaving 1 inch of stem. Return the shallots to screens and continue to dry for two to three months; then take smallest bulbs to replant for next year and store the others in baskets or mesh bags. It's better to have a number of small storage containers rather than one big one. If stored bulbs get good air circulation and cool storage temperatures of 40 to 50 degrees, they should last until your next harvest.

Bunching Onions
Allium fistulosum
Plant bunching onions in early spring for harvest through the fall, or plant in the fall for early spring use. Sow seeds 1/2 inch apart, 1/2 inch deep. You can plant three to four seeds across in a row. Harvest as you need them.

Multiplier Onions
Allium cepa, aggregatum group
Plant in the fall as you would garlic, as these onions can take around 250 days to mature. Plant 6 inches apart with the tops of the bulbs even with the soil. Mulch 2 to 3 inches on top. In spring, pull the mulch to the side and let the leaves grow tall, but cut off any flower stem that starts to form. After pulling, save some to replant.

Flowering Onions
As with the culinary alliums, most flowering onions prefer full sun. Notable exceptions are *A. moly, A. cernuum, A. triquetrum,* and *A. zebdanense,* which prefer partial shade, particularly from the afternoon sun.

Plant flowering onions somewhat shallower than other bulbs such as tulips and daffodils, at a depth one to two times the bulb diameter, depending on the climate. Soil should be well drained. All alliums need water, but these bulbs will rot in wet soil. Fertilize in spring and early fall for best flowering.

When you're deciding where to plant, remember that with many of the flowering onions, the leaves die back before the flowers appear, so they look better interplanted with other species. After blooming, most go into complete dormancy, and there will be a space in the border that you may want to fill in with annuals. Avoid planting near oriental poppies, ladyslipper, or Virginia bluebells, or the hole will appear even bigger. Any perennial with beautiful foliage will also fill in nicely; in shady areas, try some of the smaller hostas.

Plant any of the giant alliums, such as 'Lucy Ball', 'Globemaster', 'Gladiator', or *A. giganteum,* one per square foot; the medium species, five per square foot; and the small, ten per square foot. Those who want a denser look will always try to crowd in a few more, making for drama if not the best horticultural practice.

Many flowering onions reseed in the garden. I see this as a gift of nature, but if you want to keep to a more stringent plan, cut off the flower heads before they go to seed. This eliminates the opportunity to preserve the

Avid gardener Marty Rosenberg grows bunching onions in a small greenhouse in Santa Fe, New Mexico, where plants receive drip irrigation as needed.

seed heads for dried arrangements unless your timing is impeccable and you capture the seed heads after they've matured but immediately before they open. The seed heads placed in a warm, dry spot indoors will continue to open, exhibiting the seeds as part of the decoration. A few of the flowering onions such as 'Globemaster' are sterile, so there are no seeds to worry about.

The seed head on that tall stem and on others such as 'Purple Sensation' provides garden interest for many months and is a fit companion for ornamental grasses in the fall and winter garden.

Companion Plantings

Companion planting has its adherents in both folklore and science. Some plants are known to, or thought to, add beneficial elements to the soil or to repel insects and diseases that are common to other plants. They are planted not for their own sake but to ward off problems with other plants. Here are some generally agreed on do's and don'ts for planting using alliums:

- Do plant onion, garlic, chive, and leek with beet, cabbage, carrot, early lettuce, parsnip, pepper, tomato, strawberry, and chamomile. Onions may repel cabbage loopers, cabbage worms, carrot flies, and Colorado potato beetles.

- Do plant near fruit trees (but not directly underneath, because sun is usually a necessity) to help repel moles and perhaps reduce scab on apples.

Allium seed heads mix with grasses and other perennials to provide a wild and exotic look.

- Do plant near roses, as they may repel aphids.

- Do plant garlic with asters and gerber daisies to reduce fungus.

- Don't plant onions and leeks with peas, beans, or other legumes including sweet peas, or with sage or asparagus.

- Don't plant in the same row immediately following another allium crop. Use a three-year rotation schedule unless your plants are perennial.

Garlic may repel deer, birds, and Japanese beetles if sprayed on the leaves of plants. I make up a solution in my food processor with a dozen eggs, a head of garlic, and a handful of hot peppers, mixed with a little water. I spray it on foliage in the early spring when the deer are foraging among my bulbs and perennials. It's a nuisance because it must be reapplied after a heavy rain, but it seems to be effective—at least in those years when the animals aren't desperate for food. When they are desperate, nothing seems to work.

A commercial product is available consisting of garlic encased in little pegs to insert in the soil near precious plants. It worked for me for a whole season—my new tulips were left completely alone to bloom in splendor for the first time in years—but the pegs were an eyesore. The garlic is wrapped in white plastic, which stands out like a beacon among the green foliage and brown soil. Perhaps you'll find your own ingenious method of encasing garlic cloves.

Forcing Bulbs Indoors

Winters can be cold and cruel in the northern United States, and gardeners seek any method to extend the growing season in the fall and get a jump start in the winter. We buy paper white narcissus bulbs to force into bloom in December, perfuming the house for holiday festivities. We put hyacinth bulbs in small water jars and watch them pop into aromatic bloom in January. We buy pussy willow at the grand flower shows in early March to admire as the garden starts to wake up.

With a smell as sweet as lilac and an appearance like fireworks bursting in a summer sky, *Allium schubertii* is treasured by northern gardeners as a bulb for winter forcing. Hardy to zone 7, it will survive a harsh winter only if planted indoors. One November 1, I set four bulbs in a pot with seed-starting medium, planted with the tips of the bulbs about 1 inch from the surface. I watered it and put the whole thing in a plastic bag sealed with a twist tie in the

Stages in the life of *Allium schubertii*, forced into bloom on my windowsill in zone 5. Each stage has its own beauty and interest—the show is constantly evolving.

refrigerator. It stayed there through the holiday season, taking up precious shelf space that might have been better allotted to the chestnut mousse and sweet potato casserole. On February 1, I removed it, unbagged the pot, and placed it on a sunny windowsill, watering when dry to the touch. Shoots sprang up within days, and I was able to observe the fascinating process from bud development to seed head formation up close. The plant started to bloom in about three weeks and lasted about four more weeks.

Don't be surprised if the leaves start drooping as the flowers start to pop. It's nothing you did or didn't do. Like many other members of the *Allium* family, the foliage begins to droop as the flower emerges. By the time the seed head is fully set, the foliage is spent. To enjoy the plant fully on my windowsill, I trimmed a few short pieces of boxwood from my ancient evergreen shrub and "planted" them in the soil amidst the allium foliage by stripping the bottom leaves and poking the twigs in the soil about 2 inches, staying well away from the bulbs. You can use Japanese holly, lily of the valley shrub, laurel, or any evergreen you have around at the time. The boxwood cuttings stay green and fresh looking for several months and help prop up the strappy onion leaves, improving the appearance of the plant. Or you can place the pot among other house plants with strong foliage to distract from the natural course of the allium.

You can plant the same bulbs outdoors in the spring and dig them up in the fall to start the process over again, but I prefer to use fresh bulbs, because forcing often diminishes the strength of the bulb.

Windowsill Herb Gardens

For 15 years I owned and operated Meadow Lark Flower & Herb Farm in Orwigsburg, Pennsylvania. On several acres, I grew herbs and flowers for cutting and drying. Most of the crop was used for decorative work, but there was always an abundance of herbs for my kitchen. In September, I would pick what I needed for winter recipes and freeze it in carefully labeled Ziploc bags. Each spring, when my new crop sprouted, I took whatever remained in my freezer and threw it on the compost pile, because by next fall, I would have a plethora of fresh herbs to restock my supply.

Then I moved to Manhattan—no more farm, no garden, no terrace, not even a window box or a fire escape to hold large pots. An editor from *Home* magazine did me an immense favor when she asked me to write about windowsill herb gardens. I not only wrote the article but also planted some herbs to photograph on my south-facing windowsills overlooking the cityscape.

My enjoyment of cooking in my minuscule kitchen has been transformed by the selection of herbs growing on my windowsill. Right downstairs is one of the top gourmet food stores in the city, and I can purchase fresh herbs at markets when I plan a special recipe in advance, but a windowsill herb garden allows for spontaneity in cooking. Scrambled eggs can be converted into an herb omelet in 15 seconds flat. I eagerly trot about 15 feet from kitchen to windowsill with my scissors and snip off chives, thyme, and dill or any other combination for my guests or even for myself alone to enjoy. The simplest dishes become taste sensations with a little fresh basil, mint, or oregano.

Buy chives and garlic chives from a garden center or get a division from your own garden or that of a friend. Plant it in a pot with a drainage hole, with pebbles on the bottom. Remember that unglazed pots such as terra-cotta need watering more frequently, because the water evaporates through the sides of the pot. Glazed pottery or plastic pots need less attention.

Place the pot in full sun, water when the soil is dry to the touch, and keep snipping—but no more than a quarter to a third of the plant, to allow it to regrow sufficiently. Fertilize with a weak solution of organic fertilizer every two weeks spring to fall, and then ease up to once a month as the plant settles into its slow-growing winter phase. Don't fret if you lose a plant or two. Start again with a very clean pot and new soil, and try to figure out what went wrong the first time.

Favorite plants for windowsill and indoor gardens are:

- Basil *(Ocimum basilicum)*—annual

- Bay laurel *(Laurus nobils)*—tender perennial

- Chives *(Allium schoenoprasum)*—perennial

- Cilantro *(Coriandrum sativum)*—annual

- Dill *(Anethum graveolens)*—annual

- Garlic chives *(Allium tuberosum)*

- Lavender (*Lavandula* spp.)—hardy or tender perennial

- Lemon verbena (*Aloysia triphylla;* syn. *Lippia citrodora*)

- Mint (*Mentha* spp.)—perennial

- Oregano *(Origanum vulgare hirtum)*—perennial

- Parsley *(Petroselinum)*

- Rosemary *(Rosmarinus officinalis)*—tender perennial

- Sage *(Salvia officinalis)*—perennial

- Scented geranium (*Pelargonium* spp.)—grow as annual

- Thyme (*Thymus* spp.)—perennial

One Couple's Story: A Hobby Gone Wild

Does planting, weeding, and pulling 10,000 garlic plants sound like a hobby or real work? Richard and Dorothy Leach of the fertile Ringtown Valley near Shenandoah, Pennsylvania, still have their day jobs—electrician for a coal company and cutter in a sewing factory—but they're gearing up to turn their hobby into a business when they retire. In the late 1800s, when Dorothy's great-uncle immigrated from Lithuania to work in the deep anthracite mines, he brought with him 'Rocambole Porcelain' garlic to plant in the new country. It's a smallish bulb with a heavy tinge of purple, a stiff stem, and a magnificent flavor. Richard says that when it's first pulled, the fresh garlic has a sweetish taste, a little like chestnuts. By the end of the winter storage period, a more bitter flavor has developed.

The bulbs have been planted in the gardens of succeeding generations, and now the Leaches intend to preserve, protect, and develop the strain. Some folks at Rutgers University are interested in studying the medicinal properties of their strain, including the particularly high sulfur content.

Each year, the Leaches harvest "seeds" (really bulbils) against a possible crop failure. They claim that from seeds, the garlic bulbs would take four to five years to reach full size, whereas using the cloves, they can plant in September and harvest the next summer. So each year they hand-select about 1,500 bulbs with excellent color and strong roots as their mother stock. Each bulb produces six to eight cloves, which are dried and separated for replanting right after Labor Day.

The flower capsules, or top-sets, are picked from the stem when the first ones in the patch start to split open their papery covering, exposing the bulbils. The bulbs are left in the ground and continue to mature until late July or the beginning of August, when the stems are pulled by hand. The Leaches' sign to pull is when the first plants in the patch start turning brown. If left too late, when the stems are fully brown, the stems will separate from the bulbs when tugged on, requiring the use of a pitch-fork to dig up the bulbs. When first pulled, the bulbs are rinsed with a hose (something many garlic growers avoid like the plague) and left out in the sun to dry; then they are put in the shed to continue drying. The roots are cut off, but the stems are left, as they will fall off natu-rally when fully dried.

In a neat form of recycling, the Leaches find that the garlic is improved by a top dress-ing of anthracite coal ash from their furnace. Anthracite coal is still mined in the area, and many families continue to use it for heat. The Leaches' furnace is not a forced-air furnace, which leaves a residue of arsenic, mercury, and other poisons in the cinders, but a hand-fired anthracite furnace, which leaves the screened coal ash with a high sulfur and potassium con-tent and also lightens the soil with its grit. They water, if necessary from a spring.

Ringtown Valley, Pennsylvania, home to the gar-lic patch of Richard and Dorothy Leach.

Right now, the Leaches give a lot of their garlic to friends and neighbors, some of whom swear by its medicinal qualities. And they sell some to local restaurants. But when the time comes to retire, they say they'll retire into garlic.

CHAPTER SIX

Allium Crafts

ecorating the house with garlic and onion bulbs seems strange at first, but why not? The colors are subtle and lovely, the shape and textures are interesting, the price is right whether direct from the garden or from the market, and the viewer is tickled at the sight of the unexpected. And there is no smell if the bulbs are unbruised and intact. In fact, decorations can last for weeks—even months—before needing to be tossed on the compost heap.

In December 2002, we opened our home to a house tour, the Holly Trail, to benefit the local library. More than 400 people took the tour both to see five interesting homes and to see how the owners decorated their houses for the holiday season. Instead of decorating for Christmas, I decorated for a winter party. All the materials came from the garden and the supermarket—not a flower or evergreen in sight. Garlic and onions were prominently displayed, along with a dining room centerpiece of bright bell peppers on an apple stacker. I substituted the tapers in the candlestick holders with long, fresh carrots. The nonobservant walked right by without noticing; others broke into peals of raucous laughter as they caught the joke. After all, decorating for a party doesn't have to be a serious affair. The garlic swag shown on page 97 was hanging inside my front door.

LEFT: Garlic, dried allium seed heads, and a beautiful vase—it's almost everlasting.

Simple Arrangements

Among a beautiful collection of Mexican earthenware plates in a Santa Fe dining room, the onions look part of the whole. Their roundness echoes the shape of the plates. In another collection of earthenware hen casseroles, the garlic bulbs remind the viewer of eggs that might have been laid. Placed singly on a shelf, unbruised bulbs will last for many months.

When you want to make a centerpiece of something other than flowers, a bowl of onions, garlic, fruits, or vegetables is always a treat. And there's a decided bonus: The day after the party, you can sauté the centerpiece for a delicious lunch over rice or pasta.

Select a pretty, wide-mouthed bowl or plate. Stack the materials in groups. Tuck in some sprigs of berries if you have them, such as firethorn (*Pyracantha*), for extra color. Await compliments.

The earthenware here certainly needs no embellishment, but a few golden onions add warmth to the display.

Garlic cloves, less expensive and more inventive than flowers, add an interesting touch to any setting.

A design straight from the farmer's market, with a few berries tucked in.

Swags and Braids

Herb Swag

Stiff-neck garlic forms the perfect backdrop for the herb swag pictured, framing the other herbs. Although I used hot and sweet peppers for color, any available herbs can be used instead, whether culinary or not.

Hang the swag on an inside door, or outside with protection. If you have wall space in your kitchen, it looks completely appropriate, but I enjoy the incongruity of finding garlic in other rooms of the house, such as inside my front door. It will last indefinitely if it's not handled. The garlic will gradually dry, and the white husk will retain its shape and color.

WHAT YOU NEED

9 or 10 bulbs stiff-neck garlic with stems intact, cleaned, and roots trimmed

small ristra (string) dried hot peppers

2 small bunches other dried herbs (here, the gray is santolina, but sage is another excellent choice)

4 small bunches dried peppers for color

5 stems bay leaves or other green herb

florist reel wire

clippers

2 yards ribbon

WHAT YOU DO

1. On a table, lay out the garlic stems with the bulbs forming a pyramid— one at the top, and rows getting wider as you descend. The stems should flare out as well. When you have the arrangement set, wrap wire under the bulbs to secure the base of the swag.
2. Make a loop of wire in the back of the swag for hanging.
3. Hang the ristra on a nail where you want the swag to be.
4. Hang the garlic on the same nail.
5. Wire all the other herb bunches directly to the garlic base.
6. Tie the ribbon around the wrapping point, making a soft bow to hide the wire and any rubber bands holding the herbs together.
7. Stick the stems of the bay leaves into the swag among the other herbs under the wire.

Stiff-neck garlic, santolina, bay, and peppers make a welcoming decoration for your door. PHOTO BY ALAN AND LINDA DETRICK

Decorate the easy way with a ready-made garlic swag. PHOTO BY ALAN AND LINDA DETRICK

Garlic Braid Swag

Take the easy way out and purchase a plain garlic braid at a market or farm stand. Then you can have the fun of decorating it very simply as a winter door swag with little work. The braids are done very tightly, so sprigs of other materials can be tucked into the braid and will remain in place.

WHAT YOU NEED

large handful evergreen boughs (here, blue spruce); cut three to five stems, depending on how well-branched they are, 3 to 5 inches longer than the braid

garlic braid

red bow with streamers

small stems of red berries such as rose hips (as here) or holly

small stems of other silver herbs such as lamb's ears or sage

clippers

florist reel wire

WHAT YOU DO

1. Make a bunch of evergreens with the stems spread wide and flat, the tallest in the center.
2. When you are satisfied with the way it looks, bind it together at the top with the wire.
3. Make a small loop on the back with wire to hang the swag.
4. Wire the top of the garlic braid to the evergreen.
5. Attach the bow to the top of the swag, hiding all the wire.
6. Insert the sprigs of berries and herbs into the braid where they will be clasped by the garlic heads. If all else fails, you can always use a hot glue gun to attach these little pieces, but it shouldn't be necessary.

Tip: If you like a more glitzy look for the holidays, before constructing, spray the garlic braid with gold or silver paint from the hardware store. Let it dry before following the steps above. The texture of the garlic hulls makes the paint shine, and they look like large jewels.

Garlic Braid

Garlic braids, even shorts ones, include ten or more garlic bulbs. I've always been mystified by braiding more than three strands. All that practice with braiding hair, ribbons, and wool wasn't much help until I saw it done by an expert.

You can make a braid as beautiful, or let someone else do the work.

WHAT YOU DO

1. Cut the roots of the bulbs with the scissors, leaving about 1/2 inch for some textural interest.
2. Gently remove excess foliage and any hanging or damaged bulb wrappers. Removing too much of the wrapper will make the bulb fall apart, and removing too many leaves will make the stem too weak. Wipe off any excess dirt.

WHAT YOU NEED

cured garlic stems (see page 75 for curing garlic); the number of stems must be multiples of 3 plus an extra—10 is really the minimum number and will produce a small braid

scissors

natural cord

raffia strands for a bow

3. Start with two sturdy stalks. Lay them on a table, crossing the stems just under the bulb. Add a third stem on top of the two. That bulb will fall in the middle between the cross, with the bulb nestled lower than the other two.
4. Holding the three stalks together at the cross, start to braid one strand and the second as if you were braiding hair. The bulbs should never move (think of them as hair rooted into the scalp); only the stalks move. Pull gently to keep the braid tight.
5. Next, place a fourth bulb in the center of the cross. Its stem is paired with the middle stalk, and you braid them as if they were one unit. Pull gently to keep the braid tight.

6. When you are ready to add the next bulb, place it to the right of the cross, but its stem joins the center and is braided with the center strand. As each bulb is added—right, left, or center—pair the stem with the one that is now in the center.

    If you are making a long braid, the early stems will run out, but new bulbs and stems will keep the whole thing going.

7. When you are ready to finish off, continue braiding the stems without adding any additional bulbs. You can make the final braid as long as you like, but 3 to 5 inches looks nice.

8. Tie securely with the cord. Trim off the uneven ends of the braid.

9. Add the raffia tied in a bow over the tied cord, if desired.

Tip: Soft-neck garlic is easier to braid than hard-neck. If you have only hard-neck garlic, you will have to knead the stems gently with your fingers to make them more flexible.

Wreaths

Fruit Wreath with Onions

It looks complicated, but it isn't—just a little time-consuming. It's easy to do while you're watching TV, because you're just picking and sticking. Kids love to help with this project. It makes either a centerpiece or a door wreath, but it's best on a door that rarely gets opened and closed. Cool weather prolongs the life of the fruit.

WHAT YOU NEED

Styrofoam wreath ring, 12 to 14 inches diameter

round wood toothpicks and small florist picks without wire (or with the wire removed)

small fruit and onions (here, lady apples, kumquats, limes, clementine oranges, cranberries, and small purple onions; other possibilities are small, hard sickle pears, lemons, or tiny artichokes)

WHAT YOU DO

1. Place big fruits on first; then surround them with smaller fruits. Place three oranges at two o'clock, six o'clock, and ten o'clock, then two apples near each orange. The rest of the fruit can be placed randomly.

2. Stick a toothpick or florist pick into the base with at least half sticking out. Then, holding on to the pick, stick the fruit on top.

3. For cranberries, break the toothpicks in half. It may be easier to stick one end in the berry first, then the other in the wreath base.

TOP: Tiny purple onions combine with fruits for an unusual holiday wreath. BOT-TOM: The same wreath can double as a fabulous centerpiece for your holiday table.

PHOTOS BY ALAN AND LINDA DETRICK

4. If limes or lemons are too big, cut in half horizontally.

5. Remember to place fruits not only on the top surface but also inside the ring and on the exterior surface, so no Styrofoam shows. Build up the smaller fruits to make the wreath look three-dimensional.

6. Because this wreath is heavy, it should hang directly on the nail, or use it as a centerpiece.

Tip: How long the wreath will last depends on the freshness of the fruit and the temperature of your house. Buy the hardest fruit possible, and of course, it should be undamaged. Wrinkled cranberries are on their way to rotting. If you're making this wreath for the centerpiece of a party, work up to five days in advance, and place it in the refrigerator until the day of the party. You can also make it in stages this way. If you run out of time, refrigerate it and start again the next day, or place it in an unheated garage or basement.

All-Allium Wreath

This wreath is similar in structure and technique to the fruit and onion wreath, but instead of mixed fruit, it uses all small alliums, such as whole garlic heads, single cloves of large garlic, shallots, Egyptian top onions, an assortment of small onions in all colors, dried allium flowers such as chive and drumstick allium, and small seed heads of garlic chives. You also need green sheet moss to cover the Styrofoam base and a glue gun and glue sticks to secure the dried flowers and seed heads.

WHAT YOU DO

1. Follow instructions for the fruit and onion wreath, but before starting to pick and stick, cover the Styrofoam base with spots of glue and glue on the sheet moss, piecing as necessary to make it fit.

2. *Do not peel* the garlic and onions. Stick picks in the onions and garlic, starting with the largest, and stick in the wreath. Then do the same with the smaller onions and garlic cloves.

3. Glue on the dried flowers and seed heads.

Tip: The wreath will be heavy at first, then get lighter as the months pass and the alliums gradually dry out, leaving their hulls. It should last at least six months if you start with clean, unblemished garlic and onions.

This wreath emits barely any odor—just the faintest whiff as you walk by. Some of the onions and garlic may start to spout, however, and I look forward to this change. The small green shoots look lovely and enticing, a gentle reminder that you have been crafting with living things.

Arrangements of Fresh and Dried Allium Flowers

Fresh Flowers. To get the longest vase life, cut the flowers when a few florets are just starting to open. Stand them in a bucket of lukewarm water for six to eight hours to condition them. Then use the flowers in arrangements as you would any flower, mixed with other perennials, annuals, and foliage as you desire. The only time I would be leery of including allium flowers in a design is when making a bridal bouquet.

Dried Flowers. In order to dry well and hold their shape, allium flowers should be quite mature before picking. With chives, for example, I wait until the flowers are almost two weeks old and the first ones are just starting to show some little black seeds before cutting the flower stems. Bunch them in small handfuls, and secure with a rubber band. Then hang the bunches upside down from a hook in a warm, dark, dry spot. A paper clip opened to an *S* shape can be slipped under the rubber band and then hung on a hook or wire.

The flower heads dry before the stems, but chives and other small alliums dry in about two weeks; larger alliums take longer. Don't bother trying to dry the leaves, because they always yellow. When the flowers are totally dry, they can be used in design projects, or the chive flowers can be stored for culinary use.

Seed Heads. Many of the larger alliums develop wonderful seed heads after the flowers die. They provide interest in the garden, with their resemblance to imaginary planets and starry fireworks. Even garlic chives form small, tawny balls with intense black seeds atop their 20-inch stems, adding appeal throughout the winter.

Many years, I cut a few seed heads to use in everlasting bouquets and wreaths and even to decorate Christmas trees. They can be saved from year to year with other decorations, if you are so inclined.

Following are some ideas and techniques for using allium flowers and seed heads.

Ready for plucking to dry for arrangements, the fantastic seed head of *A. christophii.*

Easter Egg with Chives

Delicate mauve chive flowers are among the first flowers I cut, right after the daffodils but before the tulips. I treasure this foray into the garden, because chives are the harbinger of an awakening spring. Here, chives are teamed with wild mustard from the meadow, a handful of violets, and some stems of the perennial herb sage just reaching the bud stage. The container is a large emu eggshell (use ostrich or rhea as well, or any other small vase) with the top broken off. Eggs are watertight, and I often use clean eggshells to hold flowers. They can be washed carefully and reused indefinitely. If you happen to have a few egg cups, put clean chicken eggshells in the cups and use each to hold a small bunch of one type of flower or herb. Cluster the cups together to make a different kind of arrangement.

Cone of Fresh Flowers

Instead of the ubiquitous wreath on the front door, try an arrangement with fresh flowers and herbs in a floral cone. The cones are watertight and can hold wet floral foam in which the flowers are inserted. For longer life, fill the cone with water and insert the flowers directly. This works best on a door that is rarely opened. I have a hook next to my door jamb to hang such arrangements so door opening is never an issue yet I get the same decorative effect.

Here, the casual arrangement is made of a few branches of Scotch broom, wild mustard, flowering onion, deep blue cat mint from the herb garden, and silver leaves of lamb's ears. The selection was dictated by the few species in bloom on an early spring day.

The cone itself is covered with china shards affixed with epoxy. I had the fun of smashing chipped plates, cups, and bowls of various vintages and fitting them together like a jigsaw puzzle. Wear protective goggles when you are smashing with a hammer, and cover the china with a rag before you bang.

Chive flowers add to an early spring posey replete with wildflowers. PHOTO BY ALAN AND LINDA DETRICK

An early flowering onion, Scotch broom, cat mint, lamb's ear, wild mustard, and a few curls of Egyptian onion in a very informal display. PHOTO BY ALAN AND LINDA DETRICK

Fresh and Tight

An oval or round basket echoes the shape of the flowers in this tight arrangement. When the drumstick allium was in bloom, I searched the garden for other flowers with a similar ball shape. I found globe thistle and coneflowers for the center. Though their petals are rays, the centers were starting to mound up into beautiful golden balls.

WHAT YOU NEED

low, oval or round basket with waterproof plastic liner, or low, wide china or pottery bowl

green floral foam

paring knife

assortment of flowers

pruning shears or clippers

packet of cut flower preservative

WHAT YOU DO

1. When you bring the flowers indoors, strip all the leaves from the stems and stand them in a bucket of lukewarm water for four to six hours to condition.

2. With the paring knife, trim the foam to fit in the basket. Then remove the foam and soak it in water and floral preservative for 30 minutes.

3. Replace the foam in the basket and set aside.

Low and tight is all you need to remember to execute this simple style.

4. When the flowers have had their long drink of water, you can start making the arrangement.

5. Begin with the outside ring, using the flowers you have the most of. Cut the stems to about 4 inches. Insert the stems in the foam slanting slightly outward, covering the rim of the basket. There are 20 drumstick alliums in this 10-inch-long basket.

6. Go on to the next row. Place these flower stems slanting slightly outward as well, but higher than the first row. You are aiming for a mound effect.

7. Go on to the third row. At the top, only three coneflowers are needed to fill in the hole, because the petals spread out to cover the space.

8. With a watering can, carefully pour some additional water on the foam. Keep it well watered for the life of the arrangement, which will be almost two weeks with nice fresh flowers.

Tip: As you can see, this basket has no handle, making it a little easier to work with. If your basket has a handle, for the first row, stop at the break and continue inserting stems on the other side. After the outside row is in place, the handle won't affect the design.

Allium Everlasting

You could mix alliums with other dried flowers for more color, but this arrangement displays the subtleties of shape and texture. All you need are a few large seed heads, such as stars of Persia (*Allium christophii*); a few small seeds heads, such as the garlic chives (*Allium tuberosum*) shown here; and a few stems of hard-neck garlic (*Allium sativum ophioscorodon*). Find one tall, beautiful vase with a narrow neck, and place your materials in it.

If you have a problem balancing the vase, put some glass marbles or stones in the bottom to distribute the weight more evenly. The garlic heads are heavy until they dry, which they gradually do over six to nine months.

Other Suggestions

Use dried allium seed heads as Christmas tree ornaments. Spray them with gold, silver, or copper paint from the hardware store. One large seed head is a natural for the star on top of the tree.

Use seed heads sprayed or natural to decorate a mantel strewn with evergreens and berries. Be sure to keep them away from candles that may be lurking nearby.

A spare design can also be quite attractive.

The largest fresh alliums are out of place in most homes, but in a large room with a cathedral ceiling or in an actual cathedral, the scale of *Allium giganteum* is perfect. Mix it with branches 4 to 5 feet tall, in bud or in leaf, of regal delphinium and other bold flowers, including some exotics from the florist such as ginger or bird of paradise. Make sure the vase is well weighted with stones at the bottom for adequate balance.

Other Craft Projects

Onion Dyes for Easter Eggs

Wildflowers, fruits, and vegetables have been sources of natural dyes since humans first began to decorate the surfaces around them. Although commercial dyes are brighter and more vibrant, when planning a project with children, it's sometimes more fun and certainly more eye-opening to make your own dyes from materials you have on hand. Onion skins are perfect for the job. Yellow and purple onion skins provide two very different colors—golden brown and reddish orange, respectively.

WHAT YOU DO

1. Bring the onion skins, water, and vinegar to a boil in a stainless steel pan and simmer for 15 minutes to release the colorants. If you are using both yellow and purple onions, make two recipes in two pots.
2. If you are coloring hard-boiled eggs, simmer the eggs in the dye for 5 to 10 minutes until the desired color is achieved.
3. If you want to save your eggs from year to year, the dye bath must be totally cool before the intact raw eggs are submerged. After dying, the eggs can be pierced at the ends and blown out. If you do this first, the shells will be too light and will float in the dye bath.
4. Remove the eggs from the dye with a wooden spoon, and dry them on paper towels.
5. For a shiny finish, polish the eggs with a little cooking oil on a rag, or polish with beeswax.

WHAT YOU NEED

2 to 3 cups onion skins (save the onions for cooking later), lightly packed

6 cups water

2 tablespoons white vinegar

eggs

These eggs can be decorated in your favorite way either before or after dyeing. If the eggs are wrapped in the onion skins before boiling, and tied with string to hold the skins in place, you will get a tie-dyed look when you unwrap them.

Tip: Achieve an interesting color pattern by wrapping the eggs in the onion skins and securing them with white string. This will produce a tie-dyed effect. Unwrap one egg to test for depth of color before discarding the dye bath.

Garlic Lover's Gift Basket

For your favorite garlic lover, give a basket full of choice items. First, pile in some colorful tissue. Add a garlic press and a small ceramic garlic roaster, a few of your favorite recipes on 3x5 cards, a book on growing garlic (this one, perhaps?), some starter cloves from your own stock or a reliable source, and a few of your largest heads for cooking. Cover with cellophane and tie with raffia. Kiss the recipient after you present the basket but before the items are sampled.

Onion Printing

Printing with vegetables, fruits, leaves, and other natural elements is an age-old craft that you probably remember from childhood, but it's not only for children. Before photography, botanists used nature prints, including those of leaves, flowers, berries, and roots, to make recordings of their precious finds in far-flung sites. Other scientists made printed records of shells, fossils, and fish skeletons to record the details of new species. Currently, some print artists use natural materials to create luscious works of art.

Nature printing takes on a more sophisticated look when you use quality materials, beautiful papers, fine linens for the base, and fine paints for the stamping. You can carve a whole raw potato to create stamps to suit your artistic taste, but that requires skill with a paring knife. I prefer to let the texture of the natural material serve the purpose, and onions can speak perfectly well for themselves.

WHAT YOU NEED (for the easiest project)

several onions of various sizes, including pearl

other fruits and vegetables (optional), such as carrot, brussels sprout, mushroom, or small pepper—anything with an interesting texture when cut

paring knife

paper towels

paper for printing

stamp pads of several different colors, watercolor paints, or felt-tipped pens

WHAT YOU DO

1. Cut an onion in half through the widest part, not root to stem. Cut a slice off the bottom of a carrot, or cut a brussels sprout or mushroom in half, top to bottom. For each item, you want to expose the surface with the most interesting texture. The slice should be even, without high and low spots.

2. Wipe the cut surface with a paper towel. Onions that are very juicy may need to be blotted several times to remove all the moisture. If the onion is still too moist, leave the cut sides open in the air for about an hour to allow a dry film to form (I hope you like the smell of onions).

3. Cut the printing paper to the size you want. Some people like to print on gift wrap or stationery. For letter paper or greeting cards, you can cut and fold before you print.

4. Tearing the edges of a porous paper gives you an interesting deckle edge rather than a smooth cut. Fold and crease the paper several times, reversing the fold. Dribble a few drops of water along the fold, and allow it to sink in. Now gently rip along the fold, and the edges will pull apart, leaving the deckle edge.

5. Press your vegetable on the ink pad, then onto the paper. Use firm pressure all over, taking care that it doesn't slip or slide. You should be able to print several stamps without re-inking, which gives you an interesting variation in color tone. If you are using paint or felt-tipped pens, color the stamp, then press it on the paper. With a little practice, you will be able to get the effects you want.

For further details on more sophisticated techniques, see *Nature Printing with Herbs, Fruits and Flowers* by Laura Donnelly Bethmann.

Tip: Less ink or paint is often better than more. Too much colorant may obscure the delicate texture or pattern and can create globs. Make sure you practice first on scraps that you don't care about, but it must be the same kind of paper as your finished piece. Papers with different absorbency produce very different effects.

Onion printing can add quirky character to stationery or borders.

CHAPTER SEVEN

Cooking with Alliums

This past winter, I treated myself to a new soup cookbook containing 43 recipes with luscious photos. Only one recipe didn't require onions, leeks, garlic, shallots, or spring onions. It was a recipe for sweet summer peach soup, and a touch of garlic probably would have been a nice addition.

Every element of a meal—bread, main course, side dishes, dessert—can include garlic. Garlic mashed potatoes are becoming standard fare in restaurants, replacing the blander plain version. Chicken with 40 cloves of garlic is no longer shocking. Sometimes garlic or onions are used as flavoring to enhance the main ingredient; sometimes they *are* the main ingredient, as in creamed onions, onion soup, or caramelized spring onions.

The recipes I've included here use allium as an important ingredient, not just as a subtle hint. I've omitted desserts, though I've eaten my share of garlic fudge, garlic ice cream, and chocolate "kissed" with garlic, and I've evaluated recipes for garlic creme caramel and garlic pineapple upside-down cake. By all means, experiment by adding a clove or two of minced garlic the next time you make dessert, and decide for yourself.

Tips for Cooking with Alliums

Onions

1. To peel tiny pearl onions, drop them in boiling water for three minutes and then plunge into cold water to cool. Cut off the root end, grab at the other end, and squeeze gently to pop each out of its skin. These are now

LEFT: **Stuffed onions.**

parboiled; you can reduce cooking time in recipes such as creamed onions (see page 128) by three minutes.

2. When baking large sweet onions, cut off the top and bottom, then peel. With a sharp paring knife, make four crosscuts through the top, going down at least an inch. Scoop out a small hole in the top center for butter and seasonings. Bake covered in a shallow pan with a cup of broth or white wine for 1 1/2 hours at 300 degrees. Uncover the last 45 minutes. As the onion bakes, it will shrink slightly and separate along the cuts, producing a large flowered effect. Your favorite bread or rice stuffing, or cubed cheese and tomatoes, transforms a side dish into a delicious vegetarian main course (see page 130 for red onions with corn bread stuffing).

3. To produce a rich golden color in chicken soup without resorting to lots of fat, include skins from yellow onions along with the bulb itself. The skins will color the soup just like they dye eggs or fabrics. Of course, they are strained out along with the other limp vegetables before serving.

4. Sweet onions have a higher sugar and water content than other onions and don't store as well, but you may not cry when you cut them. For people who find that most onions disagree with them, sweet onions may be acceptable, even sliced raw on a hamburger. Try 'Sweet Texas', 'Walla Walla', 'Vidalia', or 'Veri Sweet'. The last is a new onion from Washington State, harvested from late July through September. It has less pyruvic acid than most onions, and therefore less sting and bite than even 'Vidalia'. It's great for baking and caramelizing.

Garlic

1. A new kitchen gadget that really works is the E-Z-roll garlic peeler. It's a real time-saver for recipes that call for numerous cloves. It's a small, soft plastic tube about 1 1/4 inches in diameter. You cut the bottom and top off the whole head of garlic; insert the cloves one at a time; roll the device on the counter, pressing with your hand; and the peel slips off. Amazing!

2. To roast garlic, heat the oven to 300 degrees. Cut 1/4 to 1/2 inch off the top of a whole head of garlic so the tips are exposed, but don't peel. Drizzle with a teaspoon of fine olive oil, a teaspoon of butter, or leave plain. Sprinkle with a little salt, pepper, and 1/8 teaspoon dried oregano, thyme, or

sage. Wrap in foil and roast for about 1 1/2 hours until the garlic is soft. Wait until it is cool enough to handle; then separate the cloves and squeeze one directly on a piece of crusty fresh bread to enjoy. Or squeeze all cloves into a small bowl to add to other recipes. Freeze uneaten heads in a sealed container for a week with no loss of flavor. Just warm to serve. Unglazed pottery garlic roasters work as well as foil, or maybe better, because some moisture escapes during baking, and the garlic caramelizes. To achieve the same effect with foil, carefully open the top of the foil during the last half hour of baking

3. In a container, store fresh peeled garlic cloves covered with olive oil and 1/2 cup vinegar or lemon juice. Cover and refrigerate until needed to avoid bacterial problems. You can steal a little oil for recipes as needed and replace with fresh oil.

4. Almost any meat or chicken dish tastes better with a marinade of minced fresh ginger, fresh garlic, fresh lemongrass, and lime juice. A little soy sauce lends additional flavor.

5. To eliminate the unpleasant odor immediately after eating fresh garlic, chew on an apple, parsley, cardamom seeds, coffee beans, cloves, vanilla beans, or orange peel, or swish your mouth with milk.

Roasted garlic is a perfect spread for crusty bread.

6. To remove the odor after handling garlic, rub your hands with lemon juice, vinegar, chopped parsley, or celery leaves, or add salt to any of these and rinse your hands under cool water. Bathe in hot water to reduce the aroma coming from pores.

Chives

1. Use tall, thin chive leaves to tie up vegetables into tasty bundles. Carrot sticks are ideal for this presentation, as the flavor and colors are complementary.

2. To your favorite cheese straw recipe, add 1 tablespoon chopped chives or 1 teaspoon roasted garlic.

3. Flavor butter, cream cheese, or crème fraiche with minced chives to spread on sandwiches, baked potatoes, bagels, or hors d'oeuvres.

4. Use chive stems and flowers to flavor and decorate bottles of herbal oil and vinegar, especially those given as gifts.

Leeks

1. For eating as a vegetable or baking in pies and tarts, only the white part of the leek is used, plus an inch or two of tender green stalk. Usually the tough greens are discarded, but they make a flavorful addition to soups stocks that will be strained. Sometimes I add them to a soup and just fish them out at the end, along with the whole bay leaf, woody stems of fresh thyme, and other unwanted items.

2. Because leeks are grown with the soil hilled up against the stems to keep the bottom part white and tender, they are gritty and must be well cleaned (see page 121).

Ramps

1. Cut off the roots and wash ramps well. Slip off the outer skin of the stem and wash again.

2. Both the stems and the leaves are flavorful and may be chopped and used raw or cooked. Cleaned ramps can be thrown whole into soups, but remove them at the end.

3. Some cooks prefer to blanch the ramps for a minute or so in boiling salt water to tone down the flavor, but this isn't necessary or even desirable to my way of thinking.

4. If you have extra ramps, chop them up and freeze for future use in cooked dishes.

5. Even without a recipe, ramps are a welcome addition to most stews, soups, casseroles, and meat loaves. Stuff five or six whole ramps in the cavity of a chicken before roasting and a few more between the skin and the breast to permeate the flesh while cooking.

6. Add ramps to stir-fries and such dishes as sautéed chicken breast with mushrooms.

White Bean Soup

This soup was inspired by some beautiful white beans that caught my attention in a specialty food store. Then they sat on my shelf until the leaves started to turn and my thoughts turned to autumn soups.

WHAT YOU DO

1. Soak the beans overnight in a big pot of water.
2. In the morning, drain and rinse.
3. Replace the beans in the pot with 8 cups water. Bring to a boil and simmer for 30 minutes.
4. Meanwhile, wash and peel (as appropriate) garlic, onions, carrots, celery, and parsley, and chop fine in a food processor.
5. Dump the vegetables into the pot of beans, along with the herbs and seasonings.
6. Simmer on low heat for about an hour, stirring occasionally, until the beans are tender. Remove bay leaf and woody thyme stems.

INGREDIENTS

1 pound dry white beans, flagellate type, or lima beans

8 cups water

6 or more large cloves garlic

2 onions

2 carrots

3 stalks celery

4 stems fresh parsley

1 heaping tablespoon tomato paste

3 sprigs fresh thyme or $1/2$ teaspoon dry thyme leaves

1 bay leaf

salt and pepper to taste

7. If the soup is too thick for your taste, add up to a cup of water, low-salt chicken broth, milk, half and half, or dry white wine. If adding the wine, simmer for another 10 minutes to allow the alcohol to evaporate.

Comfort food for my husband is pea soup with slices of cooked all-beef hot dogs. I indulge him by serving this bean soup the same way, and he pronounces it an acceptable substitute. Chopped ham as a garnish is also delicious.

Herbal Onion Soup

If you use canned broth but fresh herbs, this soup will taste like it was hours in the preparation, when the actual time, aside from simmering, is more like 15 minutes.

INGREDIENTS

2 cups peeled, sliced Vidalia or other sweet onions

6 cups chicken broth (I prefer low salt)

1 cup dry white wine

2 tablespoons butter or oil

2 tablespoons minced parsley

1 tablespoon minced thyme

1/2 tablespoon minced sage

ground black pepper to taste

WHAT YOU DO

1. Sauté the onions in butter or oil until golden.
2. Pour in wine, broth, and herbs.
3. Simmer 30 minutes, and enjoy the flavor. Serves 6.

Not-So-French Onion Soup

The combination of onions and cheese makes this quick soup taste French enough for most American palates.

INGREDIENTS

8 cups peeled and sliced sweet onions

2 tablespoons butter or oil

5 cups canned low-salt beef broth

2 cups water

ground black pepper to taste

6 slices stale French or Italian bread

3/4 cup shredded mozzarella or Gruyère cheese, or a mixture of the two

WHAT YOU DO

1. Preheat oven to 400 degrees.
2. Sauté the onions in the butter or oil until soft and golden, about 20 minutes.
3. Add the broth, water, and pepper, and simmer for 30 minutes.
4. While the onions are sautéing, toast the bread slices in the oven to make them crispy.

5. Ladle the soup into individual ovenproof soup bowls or ramekins. Top with a piece of toast. Divide the cheese among the six and sprinkle it on.

6. Place the bowls on a jelly-roll or broiler pan to catch any runover. Bake the bowls on the top shelf of the oven for about 10 minutes, until the cheese is melted and bubbling.

7. Pass extra grated Parmesan cheese for those who can't get enough. Beware of burnt tongues when this comes out of the oven. Serves 6.

Sweet Potato Vichyssoise

Leek and potato soup is a simple French concoction served hot or, with the addition of cream, served chilled in warm weather. Here is a delicious variation using sweet potatoes or yams instead of the starchy white boiling potatoes. If you're trying to reduce simple carbohydrates in your diet, sometimes sweet potatoes are recommended as a replacement. This soup is not only tasty but has a beautiful color which entices the palate.

INGREDIENTS

4 cups large sweet potatoes or yams, peeled and cubed

2 cups water

48-ounce can of low-salt chicken broth, or homemade broth

3 large leeks

3 cloves garlic

2 tablespoons butter

4 sprigs fresh thyme

1 teaspoon salt or to taste

minced chives or watercress

$1/2$ to 1 cup heavy cream (optional)

WHAT YOU DO

1. In a soup pot, melt the butter. Sauté the leeks and garlic in butter until limp but not brown.

2. Add the cubed sweet potatoes, water, broth, salt, and thyme.

3. Simmer until the potatoes are tender, about 30 to 40 minutes.

4. Remove the thyme stems.

5. For a smooth and creamy texture, mix in a blender, food processor, or food mill. If you don't mind bigger pieces, mash in the pot with a potato masher.

6. Serve hot or chilled with minced chives, watercress, or another favorite herb on top.

7. Just before serving, swirl in the optional cream. Serves 6 to 8.

Tip: To prepare leeks, cut off the root end and the tough greens. Use only the white part and 1 to 2 inches of tender greens. Wash and wash again. Like fresh

Sweet potato vichyssoise is an unusual twist on a classic dish.

spinach, leeks are often very sandy, and nothing is more unpleasant than chomping down on grit as you sip your soup. Wash the leeks whole, then cut them in half lengthwise and wash between the outer leaves. Slice thinly and rewash.

Dave Platt's Garlic Bread

He fed it to his baby, my beautiful granddaughter Annabelle Rose, when she was only a year old, claiming that she needed the fat for the development of brain cells. In any case, she loved to gnaw on small pieces of his flavorful garlic bread.

Place 3 tablespoons fine olive oil in a small pan. Mince or press 3 to 6 cloves of peeled garlic into the oil and warm for about 10 minutes without boiling or browning. If desired, add 1 teaspoon chopped fresh basil or oregano for additional flavor.

Slice a crusty French bread, such as a baguette, in half. Paint or drizzle the cut surface of the top half with the infused oil. Place the two halves together and wrap with foil. Bake in a 400-degree oven for 6 or 7 minutes.

Dave warns that if you're used to garlic bread made with butter, this will taste very different, partly because there is no salt in the oil. Add salt to taste if desired.

Whole Wheat Onion Cheese Bread

We have a long-standing family tradition that the youngest person in the house must sample the bread as soon as it cools and proclaim it fit for the rest of the household. My daughter Jen, the youngest of my three, was often the taster, unless a younger child happened to be at hand. In her absence, the task fell with great glee to the next brother available when the bread emerged from the oven.

On the day this onion cheese bread came from the oven, I was the youngest in the house, so the honor fell to me. I proclaimed it fit for my husband to eat and recommended that he try it toasted, which brings out the flavors of whole wheat, onion, and cheese.

INGREDIENTS

1 large onion, peeled and chopped

2 cups milk

4 tablespoons butter

2 tablespoons brown sugar or honey

1 tablespoon salt

2 packs granulated yeast

$1/3$ cup lukewarm water

$1/2$ cup wheat germ

6 cups whole wheat flour*

$1 1/2$ cups shredded cheddar cheese

WHAT YOU DO

1. Sauté the onion in 1 tablespoon butter until golden brown. At this point, all the water has evaporated. Set aside.
2. Scald the milk by bringing it just to a boil; then take it off the heat. Add the rest of the butter, salt, and brown sugar or honey. Allow the butter to melt and the other ingredients to dissolve. Pour into a big mixing bowl. Let cool to lukewarm.
3. Dissolve the yeast in the lukewarm water. When you see some small bubbles, pour it into the bowl with the warm (not hot) milk mixture.
4. Add the wheat germ and half the flour. Stir until smooth with the dough hook on your mixer or with a heavy wooden spoon.
5. Add the sautéed onions and 1 cup of the cheese.
6. Add the rest of the flour until the dough is stiff.
7. Flour a board, turn out the dough, and knead until elastic, or keep turning with your bread hook until you've reached the same point.

---

*I prefer "white whole wheat" milled by King Arthur Flour Co., Norwhich, Vermont, which is 100 percent whole wheat but lighter in color and texture than regular whole wheat. A catalog is available at 1-800-777-4434 or on-line at www.bakerscatalogue.com.

Toasting this dense and hearty bread will bring out its delicious flavor.

8. For the first rising, turn the dough into a buttered bowl, smooth side up, and cover with a clean dish towel. Let rise until doubled in bulk, about an hour.

9. Turn the dough out on the board, punch it down, and knead again. Put it back in the bowl and let it rise for the second time, until doubled.

10. Punch it down, divide the dough in half, and knead each half. Place the dough in buttered loaf pans and let it rise for the third and final time, until almost doubled. Sprinkle the rest of the cheese on the tops of the loaves.

11. Bake at 375 degrees for 40 minutes and check for a golden brown color. Bake another five minutes if necessary. Cool and slice.

Onion Tart

This tart is like onion soup in pie form, or like an onion quiche. Cut it in small wedges as an appetizer, or in larger wedges as a main course for lunch or the mainstay of a vegetarian dinner. You can bake it ahead of time and serve it lukewarm, or serve it hot just out of the oven.

WHAT YOU DO

1. Mix together the ingredients for the crust and press into the bottom of a 9-inch pie plate.
2. Sauté the onions in butter until golden brown, and spread them over the crust.
3. Reserve 1/4 cup cheese. Spread the rest on top of the onions
4. Scald the milk in a small saucepan; add salt, pepper, and nutmeg. Allow to cool.
5. Mix beaten eggs into the cooled milk, and pour the mixture over the cheese.
6. Sprinkle on chopped chives or scallions and 1/4 cup grated cheese.
7. Bake for 30 to 35 minutes at 350 degrees. Serves 8.

INGREDIENTS

For the Crust*

1 cup Ritz crackers crushed into crumbs

1/2 cup (one stick) melted butter

For the Filling

4 tablespoons butter

5 cups sweet onions, peeled and sliced thin

2 1/4 cups grated Parmesan or cheddar cheese

1 cup milk

2 large eggs, beaten lightly

1/4 teaspoon nutmeg

salt and pepper to taste

2 tablespoons fresh chopped chives or scallion greens

Welsh Leek Tart

Thanks again to Anne White Scott, my reference for all things Welsh, for this recipe. She says that this is traditionally served on St. David's Day, March 1. It was originally called kettle pie, and in the 1800s, it was made with three-cornered leeks, which grew wild.

WHAT YOU DO

1. Line a pie plate with the pastry.
2. Lightly beat the eggs with a fork, add all the other ingredients, and pour into the crust.
3. Bake for 40 minutes at 350 degrees. Serves 6 to 8.

INGREDIENTS

unsweetened short crust pastry for a 9- to 10-inch pie plate

2 2/3 cups cleaned chopped leeks

1/2 pound bacon, chopped, browned, and drained of grease

3/4 cup half and half

3 eggs

salt and pepper to taste

pinch nutmeg

*Or use your favorite prepared crust or other unsweetened crust recipe. Pre-bake for 20 minutes at 375 degrees before adding the filling.

Poached Egg Salad with Caramelized Shallots

This is a composed salad, elegantly styled for brunch or lunch. I first had a version of it at a celebratory lunch at The Dining Room on East 79th Street in New York City. It startled me with its tasty simplicity.

INGREDIENTS (for one serving)

1 egg

2 large, thin slices smoked salmon

1 shallot

1 tablespoon butter

half a seeded, diced Italian plum tomato

3 leaves Belgian endive

handful other favorite salad greens, torn (e.g., Boston lettuce, baby spinach, frisee)

1 tablespoon chopped chives

vinaigrette dressing (optional)

salt and pepper (optional)

Much of this can be prepared in advance. Then poach the eggs and add them just before serving. As you cut into the yolk, it coats the greens like a flavorful dressing.

WHAT YOU DO

1. Peel, slice, and sauté the shallot in butter until golden brown.
2. Lay out the sliced salmon on the plate, covering the bottom.
3. Cover with the endive leaves, then the caramelized shallot.
4. Sprinkle with chopped tomato, then add a small pile of well-washed salad greens, mixed with the vinaigrette if desired.
5. Poach the egg and add it last, sprinkled with the chopped chives for color.
6. Add a sprinkling of salt and pepper if you choose.
7. Serve with slices of crusty French bread lightly toasted under the broiler.

Chicken Liver Paté

Use this as an appetizer to spread on small rye rounds or as the centerpiece of a cold summer salad plate. This recipe is a spin-off of traditional chopped liver. It's quick, inexpensive, and utterly delicious.

WHAT YOU DO

1. Melt the butter in a skillet, and brown the onions.
2. Meanwhile, wash the livers in a strainer and drain. Pick over and discard any extraneous matter.
3. Peel and flatten the garlic with a large knife.

4. When the onions are browned, add the livers, garlic, sherry, salt, and pepper. Cover the pan.
5. Simmer gently for about 15 minutes, until the livers have lost their pink color.
6. Place the hard-cooked eggs in a food processor, and chop briefly.
7. Take a slotted spoon and remove the livers, garlic, and onions, and add them to the food processor. Add about 1/4 cup of the cooking liquid, and process until almost smooth. It's better if it isn't completely pureed. Taste and correct the seasoning.
8. Remove to a serving dish, and sprinkle with the chopped dill or parsley for both color and flavor.
9. Refrigerate until ready to serve. It will firm up and become a better consistency for spreading. Serves 4 on a cold plate for lunch or supper. Serves 10 as an appetizer spread.

INGREDIENTS

1 large yellow onion, peeled and chopped

1 tablespoon butter

1 pound fresh chicken liver

6 cloves garlic

1/2 cup dry sherry

1/2 teaspoon salt, or to taste

3 grinds pepper, or to taste

3 hard-cooked eggs, peeled

1 tablespoon fresh dill or parsley, chopped

Fiesta Salad

Black beans and red onions are a wonderful combination on their own. Mixing them with other bright ingredients makes your taste buds shimmy and your eyes dance.

WHAT YOU DO

1. In a bowl, mix the onion, celery, peppers, olives, and tomatoes.
2. Add the drained black beans and toss gently.
3. In a small bowl, make a dressing of the garlic, salt, pepper, cilantro, olive oil, and lime juice, and toss again.
4. Let the salad marinate, and allow the flavors to blend for an hour or two before serving.

INGREDIENTS

15-ounce can black beans, drained and rinsed

3/4 cup diced red onion

1/2 cup celery, sliced

1 cup red, yellow, or orange bell pepper (or a mixture of all three), diced

1/2 cup pitted green olives, sliced

1 pint cherry tomatoes, quartered

1 large clove garlic, minced

salt and pepper to taste

1 tablespoon cilantro, chopped

1/4 cup olive oil

2 tablespoons lime juice

Fiesta bean salad can be tossed in advance.

Tip: Other go-with ingredients are cold cooked vegetables such as corn, snow peas, shelled peas, or sliced carrots; cheddar cheese in small cubes; and diced leftover chicken or turkey. The list is almost endless. The more you add, the more dressing you may need.

Creamed Onions

In the past, when extended families lived in the same city or town, Thanksgiving dinners were mostly closed affairs. Everyone gathered around the table with someone you had known from birth. Now, looking around the table, I might see my husband's colleague who just immigrated from Cuba, along with his wife and two young children; my daughter's college friend and his partner; or my son-in-law's friend from far away.

I'm always curious about how our feast differs from others they have known, and I'm not shy about asking. For those raised in the United States, two dishes are invariably cited for their absence; string bean casserole (topped with crispy fried onions straight from the can) and creamed pearl onions. Michael MacDonald's family from New Hampshire always serves this version of the latter traditional dish. I've taken the liberty of suggesting the addition of nutmeg and chives. I find the recipe appealing because it omits the flour, which often makes creamed onions pasty.

WHAT YOU DO

1. Boil the onions until tender but firm, about 8 minutes, depending on size.
2. Drain and place in a buttered casserole dish.
3. Mix sherry, cream, salt, and nutmeg (optional), and pour over onions.
4. Dot with butter.
5. Bake covered for 20 to 30 minutes at 325 degrees.
6. Remove from the oven and garnish with chopped chives if desired. Makes a side dish for 4 to 6 people, depending on how many other dishes you are serving.

INGREDIENTS

1 pound white pearl onions, peeled

$1/2$ cup heavy cream

$1/4$ cup dry sherry

$1/4$ teaspoon salt

1 tablespoon butter

pinch nutmeg and chopped chives (optional)

Tip: The onions can be peeled, boiled, and placed in a buttered, covered casserole a day in advance and refrigerated. The following day, let them warm up to room temperature, then continue with the recipe.

Creamed onions are a necessity for many family dinners at Thanksgiving or Christmas.

Caramelized Scallions

Whether you grow your own or buy them in the market, fresh scallions or spring onions are one of the first vegetables to appear locally in season. Here's the quickest and tastiest way to prepare them as a side dish. You can also prepare them ahead of time and add a few scallions to an omelet as filling.

INGREDIENTS

2 bunches scallions, about 20 to 24

1 cup water

2 tablespoons butter

1/2 teaspoon salt

1/4 cup toasted sesame seeds*

WHAT YOU DO

1. Clean and trim the scallions, cutting off the roots and the tough greens on top, leaving about 6 inches of white and tender green. Rinse.
2. Melt butter in a large sauté pan. Place the scallions in the pan in one layer. Add the water and salt.
3. Bring to a boil and simmer uncovered for about 20 minutes, until the water is evaporated and the scallions start to brown and caramelize. This process enhances their sweetness.
4. Remove from the pan, sprinkle on the toasted sesame seeds, and serve. Serves 4 as a side dish.

Red Onions with Corn Bread Stuffing

If you ever have leftover corn bread, here's a delicious way to use it. In my household the corn bread always disappears quickly, so I have to make and hide a special batch to use for stuffing. You can substitute sweet white onions in the recipe, but the red ones make a pretty change.

WHAT YOU DO

1. Boil the onions in a pot of water until you can pierce the side with a fork, about 15 minutes. Remove and run under cold water to cool.
2. Cut a small slice off the top and bottom of each onion, then peel. The skins should come off easily. With a small knife or melon scoop, hollow out the

---

*Toasting brings out the flavor in sesame seeds. Add the seeds to the hot sauté pan before you begin the main recipe, and toast them in the dry pan for a minute or two until they turn golden. They burn quickly, so don't leave them unattended.

inside of the onion, leaving about 1/2 inch of shell. Save the scoopings for any soup or stew you may be making in the next few days. If you hold the onion in your hand, you can push the inner core right up from the bottom.

3. While the onions are boiling, toast the crumbled corn bread in the oven for about 20 minutes at 300 degrees. It should be dry but doesn't have to brown.

4. Toasting the pecans with the corn bread for the last 5 minutes brings out the flavor.

5. In a bowl, beat the egg, and add the corn bread, chopped pecans, apples, raisins, garlic, salt, and pepper.

6. Loosely fill the onion shells, mounding the stuffing at the top. Dot with butter. Place in a buttered baking dish. Add the wine-water mixture to the bottom.

INGREDIENTS

6 large red onions

2 cups corn bread, cubed or crumbled into small pieces

1/2 cup pecans, chopped or broken into big pieces

1/2 cup raisins, currants, or dried cranberries

1 cup Granny Smith apple, peeled, cored, and chopped (about 1 medium apple)

2 cloves minced garlic

1 egg

3 tablespoons butter

salt and pepper to taste

1/2 cup dry white wine and 1/2 cup water (or all water, if you prefer)

Extra stuffing from the onions, baked in a separate dish, is the cook's reward.

7. Bake in a preheated 350-degree oven for 35 to 40 minutes, until the onions are tender. This is a fine vegetarian main course for lunch or a side dish with plain roasted poultry or lamb.

Tip: Bake your own corn bread from scratch or a mix, or buy three or four corn muffins, depending on size, to use for the stuffing. This step can be done a few days ahead, as the corn bread must dry out anyway.

Pot Roast with 100 Pieces of Garlic

My husband and I are enamored of French cooking and the French language, and though I had only two years of French in high school and he only two years more, we have eaten and spoken our way through many trips to various parts of that country. One year we spent a week in a French cooking school in the Périgord, near Limoges, combining our desire to learn more about French cooking, eat fabulous meals, and practice our conversation.

Madame Fillieu-Laverne ran a restaurant in the tiny town of Abjat that was open solely *sur command* (on command—reservations made and orders taken ahead). Several times a year, she welcomed eight students to stay at her home, where each morning she gave us the menu with recipes, and we watched as she prepared the evening meal. While it was cooking or baking, we went off to explore the countryside, reassembling in the kitchen for a glass (or two) of wine before dinner while she completed last-minute preparations. The third morning, Madame shocked the class by proposing a pot roast with *cent pieces d'ail* (100 cloves of garlic). This was well before any of us had heard of Julia Child's recipe for roasted chicken with 40 cloves of garlic, so we were astonished by the idea.

She browned the roast and added onions, tomatoes, brandy, and a traditional fresh herb bouquet of thyme, parsley, bay, and tarragon. Meanwhile, the class peeled the garlic cloves, which were added over, under, and around the roast. We were laughing and joking about what we would find at the end of the day, but much to our relief and surprise, the slow cooking at a low temperature caused the garlic to completely lose its bite, and it dissolved to thicken the pan juices. My mouth is watering as I write these paragraphs, and my husband is calling for an encore.

Spring Rice Pilaf with Ramps

Welcome spring with a zesty pilaf flavored with the best of the early crop of herbs and vegetables. Ramps can be used by the handful to season almost any dish, but here they are combined with an assortment of mushrooms and served with an accompaniment of grated Parmesan. Similar combinations can be featured in a traditional risotto, where the rice is cooked with cream and butter and flavorings added. Here I've cut the calorie cost, but not the flavor, by using no cream and only a minimal amount of butter. Select white or brown rice for this dish, according to your preference.

INGREDIENTS

2 cups rice

4 cups boiling water

4 tablespoons butter

$^{1}/_{2}$ teaspoon salt

ground pepper to taste

15 ramps, more or less, to taste

2 medium onions, peeled and chopped

$^{1}/_{2}$ pound assorted wild or cultivated mushrooms, washed, trimmed, and sliced

1 cup dry white wine, such as Muscadet

grated Parmesan cheese

Early spring ramps inspire a tasty rice pilaf.

WHAT YOU DO

1. Sauté the onion in 2 tablespoons butter until golden.
2. Stir in the rice until coated with butter. Add salt and pepper.
3. Pour in the boiling water, cover the pan, and simmer for 20 minutes. Then turn off the light and let it sit for at least 15 minutes to absorb the rest of the water. Don't lift the lid during this process. The steam helps the rice finish cooking.
4. Meanwhile, prepare the ramps. Wash carefully, cut off roots, and slip outer skin off stems. Cut off leaves and reserve. Chop the stems and leaves, but keep them separate.
5. Sauté the mushrooms in the remaining butter for about 10 minutes until cooked, and add the chopped ramp stems. Cook another minute or so, then pour in the wine and reduce. The mushrooms and ramps should be ready about the time the rice is finished.
6. Fluff the rice with a fork, pour the mushroom mixture on top, and sprinkle on the chopped, uncooked ramp leaves.
7. Serve with grated cheese for each diner to add as desired. Serves 4 as a main course for lunch with a salad and crusty bread or as a side dish with dinner.

This is the kind of recipe to which almost anything can be added. Try spring asparagus cut into 1¹/₂-inch pieces; fiddleheads from early ferns; leftover cubed chicken, turkey, or ham; other sautéed vegetables, such as grated carrots or sliced celery; and parsley, mint, or thyme for additional seasoning. Instead of rice, substitute bulgur (cracked wheat) to make a pilaf with a slightly different flavor.

Sweet-and-Sour Onions and Veggies

Sweet-and-sour dishes are found in many classic cuisines, from Chinese to Vietnamese to Filipino Italian. Sweet-and-sour sauces are used on everything from meatballs, spare ribs, swordfish, and carp to fiddleheads, Brussels sprouts, beets, and leeks. Recipes usually combine vinegar with white or brown sugar to produce two seemingly incompatible flavors that burst on the tongue simultaneously. I prefer to use lemon juice for the sour part of the recipe, adding a fruity tone to the acid.

My mother made sweet-and-sour stuffed cabbage leaves, in which a quarter pound of ground meat was stretched to flavor about 4 cups of cooked rice stuffed into the large leaves from one head of cabbage. These inexpensive ingredients combined to form the main course for six people. The stuffing also included golden raisins, chopped onions, and an egg or two to hold it together. The cabbage rolls were gently simmered in a fragrant mixture of tomatoes and more chopped onions, flavored with brown sugar, lemon juice, salt, and pepper. Mother claimed that the flavor

INGREDIENTS

3 cups small white boiling onions, peeled

5 to 6 peeled, sliced carrots

handful of other vegetables, such as miniature squash or snap peas, for color

3 tablespoons butter

3 tablespoons lemon juice

2 teaspoons brown sugar

water

salt and pepper to taste

was even better the next day, but as I recall, there were never any cabbage rolls left to put her theory to the test.

Use sweet-and-sour onions as a side dish with roasted chicken, beef, pork, ham, or lamb, or with broiled chicken breasts or chops. I served the dish on a hot July evening with cold poached salmon sprinkled with chopped dill and sorrel, and that wasn't bad either. When guests ask for a second helping of vegetables, you know you're on to something.

WHAT YOU DO

1. Melt the butter in a large saucepan. Add the onions and carrots in a shallow layer.
2. Add the lemon juice, brown sugar, salt, and pepper.
3. Add an inch of water to the pan.
4. Simmer on low heat for 30 minutes, being careful not to let all the water evaporate. If it does, add a little more.
5. Add the squash and continue to simmer for another 30 minutes. Peas would be added after 45 minutes.
6. After about an hour, taste and correct the seasoning. Let the water cook down, and carefully allow the veggies to brown slightly before serving them with the juices. Serves 4 to 6.

Tip: The only complicated part is peeling the onions. See page 116 for a tip that makes this step easy.

Bialys

No book about onions would be complete without a bow in the direction of the bialy, a round yeast roll with soft, puffy sides and a crisp crust that features chopped onions in its concave center and poppy seeds sprinkled on top. When I was a girl, bialys rivaled bagels in popularity at the Sunday morning breakfast table, and members of the *mishpoka* (extended family) were known by their preferences in the bialy-bagel wars.

But times have changed, and the bagel has morphed into a soft, round lump of dough with a hole in the center. No longer boiled and then baked, as in the olden days, it is shot with preservatives, baked, and sent to the shelves, where it can languish for days and still remain soft. Under many labels, the chewy quality is extinct, and the flavor is gone.

Bialys never reached that sort of popular acclaim and concomitant ruination. In New York City, at least, they remain more true to form, although sometimes the poppy seeds are sparse or missing completely. Sometimes the onions are sautéed in oil, sometimes they are replaced altogether by garlic, and sometimes the bialy is naked. I've even heard of but never seen questionable additions such as raisins and cinnamon.

The original name of bialy was *Bialystoker kuchen* in Yiddish, and devotees were called *Bialystoker kuchen fressers* (people who gorged on bialys). The recipe seems to have originated in the town of Bialystok, close to the Russian-Polish border, which was part of Russia until after World War I, then part of Poland.

My paternal grandmother immigrated from Bialystok at age two in 1879 with her parents. My maternal great-grandfather immigrated in 1912, long after the rest of the family. At age 92, he sold from a pushcart in Brooklyn until his death at age 94.

I imagine my family savoring their hot bialys at home in Russia. Then I imagine the memory of sweet onions atop the soft yet crispy rolls accompanying them across Europe and the Atlantic Ocean, into the enclave of immigrants who craved a taste of home in Brooklyn.

Mimi Sheraton, the eminent food critic and historian, has written a delightful book entitled *The Bialy Eaters,* in which she traces the origins and history of this beloved bread. Sheraton gives an elaborate recipe and instructions for the home baker, to which I refer you.

But if you're not of a mind to do it yourself, the next time you are in New York City or any large industrial city between there and Chicago, search them out anywhere kosher bakery items are sold, and try one smeared with cream cheese or butter. They're hard to toast because the onions might burn, but warm and fresh from the bakery, they need no toasting. Whether you slice across to make a sandwich, smear the butter or cream cheese on the bottom so as not to dislodge the onions, or spread it on the top, your favorite way to eat bialys depends on the way you grew up. The foods from one's childhood assume a mystical quality that latecomers cannot possibly appreciate. But without the onions, bialys would be nothing.

Garlic Festivals

Notrth, south, east, and west—from Delray Beach, Florida, to Vermont, from Pennsylvania to Gilroy, California; from Ontario to British Columbia—garlic festivals attract amateur cooks and professional chefs, serious gourmands and *fressers* (snackers). People stock up on a year's supply of their favorite natural pharmaceuticals or their favorite herbs. Some are looking for a fun day in a fairlike atmosphere full of music, dancing, crafts, lectures, demonstrations, and lore. The Gilroy Garlic Festival boasts 120,000 people in three days; others are much smaller one-day affairs, but if you've never tasted chocolate-covered garlic, you've got to go.

The Pocono Garlic Festival happens each year on the Saturday before Labor Day in front of the Monroe County Courthouse (built in 1890) in Stroudsburg, Pennsylvania. The crowd is a little sparse in the morning, because many people feel that 10 A.M. is too early to start dosing oneself with garlic. By lunchtime, the serious eating starts. In the crisp, clear mountain air, you have a choice of garlic pretzels, plain or with sesame- or garlic-filled braids; garlic pita crisps; grape leaves with garlic, hummus, and baba ghanouge; gyros and tyropita cheese pies, well laced with garlic; kielbasa sausage with a strong garlic infusion; Polish pierogies with garlic butter; hot dogs with garlic chili; and turkey barbecue with roast garlic. If that weren't enough, you can start with roasted garlic chowder and end with chocolate fudge "lightly kissed" with garlic. There are also bottles of garlic vinegar to take home. A local winery, Big

LEFT: *A. unifolium,* an heirloom species suitable for rock gardens or low borders.

A six-foot braid of garlic from Cayuga Garlic Farm in New York.

Creek Vineyards, has a stand, so you can wash the whole thing down with one of its best cabernets. Of course, you can buy heads of garlic, but to help you slice, press, and roast, there are gadgets for each operation. And to top it off, what every person needs—soaps and massage oils infused with garlic to make yourself irresistible. Before leaving, we nibbled on fresh cloves of garlic dipped in sweet milk chocolate. These can knock your socks off and are meant for die-hard fresh garlic fans only.

At the Hudson Valley Garlic Festival in Saugerties, New York, 100 beautiful miles upriver from New York City, you might be greeted by the Garlic Goddess herself, Pat Reppert, who is adorned in full regalia: turban, headdress, and garlic clove earrings. She has just come to the festival grounds from the garlic parade through the main street of Saugerties. You must see garlic-themed floats to appreciate the creativity involved in the process. Whether you are looking for new varieties, organic products, or a 6-foot braid of 'German White', you can find it here. Each half hour the music changes—dulcimer competes with zydeco, fiddlers with youth dance groups. A horticultural lecture on saving seed stock competes with one on garlic lore. Performers and lecturers on five stages struggle for the attention of the garlic lovers who are busy eating their garlic steamed clams and garlic roasted corn.

The Ramps Festival is nearing its fiftieth year in Cocke County, Tennesee. High in the

Great Smoky Mountains, it celebrates the harvest of wild ramps. In early May, they have a beauty pagent crowning the "Maid of the Ramps," and both the avid and the uninitiated enjoy ramps in all forms, along with smoked charcoal chicken, corn bread, and pinto beans, washing it all down with sassafras tea. Bluegrass music mingles with aromas wafting from the makeshift grills and stoves, and a good time is had by all.

Here's a partial list of festivals in the United States and Canada and their current contact information, listed by date, from earliest to latest. This information changes all the time, so check before you go. A useful update on many current festivals can be found online at www.garlicfestival.com. This site has links to the individual festivals.

Ramps Festival, Cocke County, TN: early May
www.cockecounty.com/activities/festivals.htm

Garlic Festival, Fairfield, CT: early May
Notre Dame Catholic School, 203-372-6521

Northwest Garlic Festival, Ocean Park, WA:
   mid-June
Cathy Marshall, 360-665-4529; or Ocean
Park Chamber of Commerce

Gilroy Garlic Festival, Gilroy, CA: last full
   weekend in July (three days)
www.gilroygarlicfestival.com

Arlington Garlic and Music Festival, Arlington, WA: second weekend in August
Ammishaddai Isreal, 360-435-8577

Garlic butter on fresh corn—a favorite from the garlic festival.

Garlic Festival in the West, Filaree Farm, Okanogan, WA: end of August
509-422-6940; www.filareefarm.com

Pocono Garlic Festival, Stroudsburg, PA: first weekend in September
570-421-7235 or 610-381-3303

Southern Vermont Garlic and Herb Festival, Wilmington, VT: first weekend
    in September
Joy and Steve, 802-368-7147

Garlic Festival of Kootenays, BC: early September
Maggie Bajer, 250-265-4967

Garlic Festival and Smoked Foods Extravaganza, Atlantic Brewing Co., Bar
    Harbor, ME: mid-September
Kate Caivano, 207-288-2337

Hudson Valley Garlic Festival, Saugerties, NY: last full weekend in September
Pat Reppert, chair; www.hopefarm.com/garlic.htm

Virginia Wine and Garlic Festival, Amherst, VA: mid-October
Richard Hanson, 804-946-5168

Delray Beach Garlic Festival, Delray Beach, FL: first weekend in November
www.dbgarlicfest.com

Garlic Is Life (festival and annual symposium on health benefits, cooking,
    and growing): first weekend in November
email@garlicislife.com or www.garlicislife.com

Sources

Culinary Allium Seeds, Sets, and Bulbs

Filaree Farm
182 Conconully Highway
Okanohan, WA 98840
www.filareefarm.com

Garden Medicinals and Culinaries
PO Box 320
Earlysville, VA 22936
www.gardenmedicinals.com

Garlic Seed Foundation
c/o Rose Valley Farm
Rose, NY 14541-0149
Nonprofit organization dedicated to improving garlic and its production. Newsletter called The Garlic Press *for small commercial growers includes news about research, workshops, farm tours, grower days, and garlic festivals.*

Gourmet Garlic Growers (Texas)
www.gourmetgarlicgrowers.com

Irish Eyes and Garden City Seeds
(Washington State)
877-733-3001
www.irish-eyes.com
e-mail: potatoes@irish-eyes.com

Richters Herb Nursery
Ontario, Canada
905-640-6677
www.richters.com

Sandy Mush Herb Nursery
316 Surrett Cove Road
Leicester, NC 28748-5517

Seed Savers Exchange
3076 North Winn Road
Decorah, IA 52101
www.seedsavers.org

Area codes change frequently. If you have trouble reaching a number, please check for new area code.

Southern Exposure Seed Exchange
PO Box 170
Earlysville, VA 22936
804-973-4703

Territorial Seed Co.
PO Box 157
Cottage Grove, OR 97424-0061
541-942-9547
www.territorial-seed.com

Well-Sweep Herb Farm
908-852-5390

Flowering Allium Bulbs

Brent and Becky's Bulbs
877-661-2852
www.brentandbeckysbulbs.com

John Scheepers, Inc.
860-567-0838
www.johnscheepers.com

Van Bourgondien
800-622-9997
www.dutchbulbs.com

Van Dycks Bulbs
800-248-2852
www.vandycks.com.

White Flower Farm
800-ALL-BULB
www.whiteflowerfarm.com

Heritage Plant and Seed Specialists

Antique Rose Emporium
800-441-0002
www.antiqueroseemporium.com

Bountiful Gardens
18001 Shafer Ranch Road
Willits, CA 95490
707-459-6410

David Austen Roses
800-328-8893
www.davidaustenroses.com

Heirloom Roses
503-538-1576
www.heirloomroses.com

Historical Iris Preservation Society
www.worldiris.com

Landis Valley (PA) Museum
Heirloom Seed Project
717-569-0401

Seeds of Change
505-438-8080
www.seedsofchange.com

Select Seeds—Antique Flowers
800-653-3304
www.selectseeds.com

Shepherd's Seeds
860-482-3638
www.shepherdseeds.com

Further Reading

Angier, Bradford. *Field Guide to Wild Medicinal Plants.* Mechanicsburg, PA: Stackpole Books, 1978.

Bethmann, Laura Donnelly. *Nature Printing with Herbs, Fruits and Flowers.* Pownal, VT: Storey, 1996.

Crawford, Stanley. *A Garlic Testament: Seasons on a Small New Mexico Farm.* Albuquerque: University of New Mexico Press, 1998.

Damrosch, Barbara. *Theme Gardens.* New York: Workman Publishing, 1982.

Davies, Dilys. *Alliums: The Ornamental Onions.* Portland, OR: Timber Press, 1992.

Drzewucki, Vincent Jr. *Gardening in Deer Country.* New York: Brick Tower Press, 1998.

Duke, James A. *The Green Pharmacy.* Emmaus, PA: Rodale Press, 1997.

Elias, Thomas S., and Peter A. Dykeman. *Edible Wild Plants: A North American Field Guide.* New York: Sterling Publishing, 1990.

Engeland, Ron L. *Growing Great Garlic.* Okanogan, WA: Filaree Productions, 1991.

Grieve, Mrs. M. *A Modern Herbal.* Vols. 1 and 2. New York: Harcourt Brace, 1931.

Heffner, Sarah Wolfgang. *Heirloom Country Gardens.* Emmaus, PA: Rodale Press, 2000.

Jones, Evan. *The Life and Times of James Beard.* New York: Alfred A. Knopf, 1990.

Kirkpatrick, Debra. *Using Herbs in the Landscape.* Mechanicsburg, PA: Stackpole Books, 1992.

Kowalchik, Claire, and William Hylton, eds. *Rodale's Illustrated Encyclopedia of Herbs.* Emmaus, PA: Rodale Press, 1987.

Kuhn, Merrily A., and David Winston. *Herbal Therapy and Supplements.* Philadelphia: Lippincott, 2000.

Lawrence, Valerie, et al. Garlic, effects on cardiovascular risks and disease, protective effects against cancer and clinical adverse effects. Agency for Health Care Research and Quality, U.S. Department of Health and Human Services, 2000.

Lehner, Ernst, and Johanna Lehner. *Folklore and Symbolism of Flowers, Plants, Herbs and Trees.* New York: Tudor Publishing, 1960.

Moldenke, Harold N., and Alma L. Moldenke. *Plants of the Bible.* Waltham, MA: Chronica Botanica, 1952. Reprint, New York: Dover, 1986.

National Audubon Society. *Field Guide to North American Wildflowers.* New York: Alfred A. Knopf, 1995.

Platt, Ellen Spector. *Flower Crafts.* Emmaus, PA: Rodale Press, 1993.

———. *Lavender: How to Grow and Use the Fragrant Herb.* Mechanicsburg, PA: Stackpole Books, 1999.

———. *Lemon Herbs: How to Grow and Use 18 Great Plants.* Mechanicsburg, PA: Stackpole Books, 2002.

Rivlin, Richard S. "Historical Perspective on the Uses of Garlic." *Journal of Nutrition* 131 (2001): 951S–954S.

Sheraton, Mimi. *The Bialy Eaters.* New York: Broadway Books, 2000.

Strouhal, Eugen. *Life of the Ancient Egyptians.* Norman: University of Oklahoma Press, 1992.

Index